PERSONAL POWER
THROUGH
AWARENESS

Books by Sanaya Roman

EARTH LIFE SERIES
Living with Joy:
Keys to Personal Power & Spiritual Transformation

Spiritual Growth: Being Your Higher Self

SOUL LIFE SERIES
Soul Love: Awakening Your Heart Centers

BOOKS BY SANAYA ROMAN AND DUANE PACKER, PhD
Opening to Channel: How to Connect with Your Guide

Creating Money: Attracting Abundance

PERSONAL POWER THROUGH AWARENESS

A Guidebook for Sensitive People

Revised Edition

An Orin Book by

Sanaya Roman

H J Kramer
a division of

New World Library
Novato, California

H J Kramer

a division of

New World Library
14 Pamaron Way
Novato, California 94949

Text design by Tona Pearce Myers

Library of Congress Cataloging-in-Publication Data

Names: Orin (Spirit), author. | Roman, Sanaya, Medium.
Title: Personal power through awareness : a guidebook for sensitive people /
[channeled by] Sanaya Roman.
Description: Revised edition. | Novato : New World Library, 2019.
Identifiers: LCCN 2018048515 | ISBN 9781608686070 (print : alk. paper)
Subjects: LCSH: Spirit writings. | Self-realization--Miscellanea. | Telepathy.
Classification: LCC BF1301 .O72 2019 | DDC 133.9/3--dc23
LC record available at https://lccn.loc.gov/2018048515

First printing of revised edition, June 2019
ISBN 978-1-60868-607-0
Printed in Canada on 100% postconsumer-waste recycled paper

New World Library is proud to be a Gold Certified Environmentally Responsible Publisher. Publisher certification awarded by Green Press Initiative. www.greenpressinitiative.org

10   9   8   7   6   5   4   3   2

Contents

Section II. Clearing Energy

SECTION I

Sensing Energy

CHAPTER I

Greetings from Orin

I invite you to explore with me the Universe you know so well. We will view it from a slightly different perspective, in a way that allows it to take on an added dimension, an unsuspected richness. It is the world of energy that exists all around you.

This book will enable you to see more clearly the energy world you exist in, to understand the belief systems, mass consciousness thought forms, and telepathic energies of others that may be affecting you. It is a course in bringing the unconscious into consciousness, delving into the mystery of the unseen energies in and around you. There is much beyond what you perceive with your five senses, and it can affect you. When you understand these unseen energies, you can stop letting them affect you.

Looking at energy closely is like looking at a familiar object through a microscope. Although it is still the same object, it looks different up close. This course will act like a microscope, helping you view the unseen energies around you in greater detail, turning and adjusting the focus to provide a different perspective. It is the same world you have always known, but as you understand and perceive it in new ways it will reveal some of its secrets to you.

You can learn to recognize the energies
you pick up subconsciously.

The microscope, in this case, is your awareness, your innate ability to focus your attention on whatever you choose. Not only do you perceive the world through your physical senses, you also pick up information constantly at a nonverbal, intuitive level. Your thoughts are the doorway to sensing energy, and your inner eyes provide the perception needed to change and work with the energy you sense.

You can learn to stop letting negative energy affect you, increase your ability to visualize, and have telepathic communication with people, knowing how to work with their nonverbal messages. You will be working with your inner world. Part of sensing energy is hearing the messages all around you. You need not be affected by other people's bad moods. You have the ability to increase the positive energy around you and change the nature of your personal relationships.

You are like a radio that can receive
many stations. What you receive
depends on what you pay attention to.

Many energies exist that can affect you throughout the day. Besides receiving energies that are all around you, you are also a broadcasting station, with a home base, a frequency, and a mind-set. The way you perceive, judge, and react to your thoughts throughout the day grounds you in your reality and is the basis upon which that reality is created.

As you become thoroughly familiar with your reality, you can choose to leave it, for there are many realities you may step into once you are familiar with your own home station. You have a greater identity than you can imagine; you can unlock your present identity to experience even more of the richness of who you are.

Because you are like a radio receiver, you can learn to set the dial and receive whatever information you want. You are telepathic — you receive and send messages all the time. In this book you will learn how to control the messages you pick up, choosing what you want to hear and letting go of broadcasts you do not want to receive. You will discover how to tune in to other people's energies to assist them in expanding into more light and love as you learn to respond from a place of greater love and understanding.

If you want to become successful, if you want to experience greater peace and love between yourself and other people, if you want to move out of the denser energies and into the finer ones, you can learn to do so.

You can learn to identify the thoughts and feelings of others you do not want to tune in to, turning off their broadcasts and linking with the higher energies of the Universe instead. You can open your intuition, that ability to sense and understand events at a deeper level, and, from your higher self, receive guidance and answers to your questions.

I have presented the information and concepts in this book in a way that will help you open to a deeper part of your being, triggering the memory of this and much more knowledge that already resides within you. You may experience my energy behind the words, which will help bring out the buried knowledge in you, awakening parts of you that have been slumbering. You meet these parts of yourself frequently in your dream state, and you can bring them into your normal, waking consciousness.

Humanity is awakening many new abilities. These abilities are part of the evolutionary journey of humanity. The human aura — the energy surrounding the body — is evolving. With this evolution comes the ability to sense what used to be unseen, invisible energy. People can now recognize, interpret, and work with that energy; that which was unseen and unrecognized can now be visible and known.

You are evolving rapidly, and the evolutionary journey of humanity is continuing to take a leap forward. When you look back into the days of the Neanderthals and Cro-Magnons, you can see that the human body has changed. People's ability to sense energy has changed as well. Even the five senses have changed. For instance, earlier humanity did not have the ability to see all the colors you can see today.

Your energy centers are opening.
Your ability to be aware of
previously invisible
and unseen energies is increasing.

You can learn how to use these newly awakened senses. They are already awakening and present in you, or you would not feel called to this information. I am acting as a guide, one who has traveled before in these realms of energy that you are beginning to explore.

Things such as telepathy, precognition, the ability to tap into new scientific inventions, discoveries of information not yet known, and an increased connection with universal consciousness will become the norm as evolution takes its course. The awakening of humanity is a journey into awareness of the higher energy realms.

It is now possible for many to learn what was previously only possible for a few. The awareness that used to take years of training in special techniques and meditation to develop is now achievable without years of special preparation. The evolutionary journey is one of awakening consciousness.

I will help you in this book to discover, understand, and nurture the awakening that is already present within you. If you feel drawn to this information, then you are certainly developing and experiencing these latent abilities. You can use them to operate more efficiently in your everyday world.

Many of you grew up as aware, sensitive children.

Many of you may have grown up in environments that often seemed inexplicable, experiencing situations that did not seem to match who you are. Some of you felt different from those around you, as if you had an added dimension of awareness that other people did not have.

Many of you felt emotionally sensitive, and it may have seemed that things that did not bother other people affected you greatly. You often did not know what was you and what was other people. Because you were telepathic and emotionally sensitive, you may have taken in other people's feelings and emotions and thought they were your own.

Most of you are gentle, loving, and sensitive, wanting to develop your personal power in ways that honor both yourselves and others. Many of you had painful childhoods, not understanding how to deal with the rigidity or negativity you found around you. Often the people you were around did not recognize you for who you are — a being of light and love wanting an opportunity to spread your joyful abundance of spirit. You who are evolving this new "6th sense" are on an accelerated path of growth and need to discover and appreciate your uniqueness and skills.

*As you open, it is important
to develop wisdom, release pain,
and rise above negativity.*

As you begin sensing and interpreting the subtler and unseen energies of the Universe, you will be developing the skill to know which energies to let become a part of you and which to release. You can connect with your higher self and soul to rise above and be unaffected by the pain and negativity in other people, as well as to receive the guidance that your higher self is always offering you.

You can open to your greater consciousness, travel into dimensions and realms that you have not yet explored, and perceive yourself in larger and expanded ways. You can learn to recognize and understand who you really are and begin to find answers to questions such as "Who am I?" and "What am I?" As you explore and awaken to these subtle energies, many doors will open and many new worlds will be there for you to discover.

I invite you to explore your greater being and to use your sensitivity to know the magnificence of who you are. Join with me. Explore all the possibilities that lie ahead as we journey together into the higher realms of the Universe.

In love and light,
Orin

Sensing Energy

A s you read this, sit in a comfortable position. Use every sense you have. Feel your breathing in your chest, face, mouth, and throat. You have many faculties for sensing energy; it is only a matter of paying attention to them. For a moment, listen to every sound in the room and outside of it. Become aware of your sense of smell, of touch, of the feeling of the clothing on your body, of what you are sitting on. Pay attention to any taste in your mouth. Close your eyes and think of all the things you have looked at today, as if everything you saw were in a movie you had seen. What pictures did you put on your movie screen today?

Besides these familiar senses, you have another faculty you use all the time — your ability to sense energy. You use it whether you are consciously aware of it or not. You make decisions based upon the energy you sense. As you closed your eyes to think of the things you saw today, you used a process called visualization. You ran a movie inside your mind, reliving and seeing again what happened. In the same way, you can close your eyes and think of a rose, imagining that you smell its delicate fragrance, envisioning the color and the shape of it. You can picture sticking out your tongue and tasting it. All of this happens inside your mind. The ability to sense energy comes from the same place.

Each of you has the ability to visualize, for I believe everyone can think of a rose, either to picture it or to feel it. This is the process you will use to become aware of the energy you live around. You can learn to feel the emotional energy in a room of people, picking out which person is emitting energy that feels like anxiety, upset, or joy. You can learn to change the effect that energy might have on you by focusing with precision on the energy that is bothering you, and learning how to tune it out.

The process of visualization can transform energy from negative to positive.

Just as you can close your eyes and visualize a rose, so can you use the process of visualization to change energy that you do not like or would like to shift. It is a process of becoming aware of your inner being. You have what I call inner eyes. You will use your inner eyes to sense energy. Your inner vision can work in many different ways. Some of you are able to picture the rose; some of you simply have a sense of it. Each of you has your own method of visualizing energy; there is no one right way to sense it.

To be able to sense energy, you need to be aware of your own energy and be able to clear your mental and emotional slate. If you saw a movie on a screen that had many crayon marks on it, the image on the screen would be jumbled rather than clear. To read energy, first clear your inner screen. For a moment, close your eyes and imagine that you have a clear white screen in your mind.

A simple exercise to do before you sense energy is to take a deep breath and imagine a clear light from the Universe coming straight down from above, into your head, all the way down through your body and out through your feet. Then picture that energy arising from the bottom of your feet, going up through the top of your head and out into the world, clearing your energy as it moves through you. Picture light spreading throughout your body. Notice if you feel lighter and freer. This is an exercise for relaxation and clearing, for it is only when you are relaxed and in peaceful emotional and clear mental states that you can sense energy clearly.

Tension in any form obscures clarity and blocks telepathic reception. Negative emotions will block an accurate picture. In fact, if you are feeling any negative energy when you begin to sense energy, this will draw negative energy to you from others.

Clear yourself out by creating a state of relaxation and peace. Your image of the white screen will create the state of mind that you need, and deep breathing will clear your emotions. Practice creating a state of relaxation. You can do it in a quick moment. If you walk into any place — an office, a restaurant, a grocery store — where you sense the energy is not to your liking, do not allow that energy to activate the part of you that does not like it. That would increase its effect on you.

Most of you tense up when you encounter negative energy. That attracts even more energy that is negative. To avoid being affected by negative energy, relax. Any process of relaxation will work. Then visualize or imagine a peaceful feeling. By imagining and then experiencing the feelings you want, you will not pick up negative energy.

Suppose you walk into a room and you are thinking of a person you are angry with, or you are lost in thoughts of something else. You are not in present time or aware of your surroundings. The emotions that go along with your thoughts will magnetize similar emotions from people around you. If you walk into a restaurant and you are feeling bad about something you did, fairly soon you will feel even worse. For just as if you were a receiving station, you will connect with everyone in the room who is feeling the same emotional energy and pull it into yourself.

On the other hand, you can, if you want, use group energy to go to higher levels of thought or emotion. Try walking into a theater, restaurant, office, or grocery store with wonderful thoughts. You will begin to connect with the wonderful feelings of those around you, which will magnify your own ability to feel good. You will amplify others' good feelings as well.

*In every home are
the energies and thoughts
of the occupants.*

What effect do people have when they walk into your home? Most visitors in your home add to the positive energy in it, for most people focus on those things that they like and admire. However, if critical people come in and think, "How ugly this is, how bad this is," they contribute to the negative energy in your home. Be aware of what kind of people you invite into your home.

Every object in your home, and your home itself, is charged with your thoughts and energy. Every time you look at your house and think, "This is too small; I do not like it," you send that energy into your house. It will be there to help bring you down. Every time you say, "What a wonderful place I live in; how fortunate I am to have this place," you make your home your friend and ally. Then, at times when you are not feeling good, you will find solace and comfort in your home. Hating something ties you to it, and if you want to move to a better place, start by loving what you have.

Watch how you respond when you handle the mundane things that come up every day. Every time you tense up when a light bulb goes out, or get upset when your car makes a strange noise, you create tension that becomes like a magnetic force and draws to you the next wrong thing.

Tension or upset in your body can magnetize more problems to you. If, when you first hear a strange noise in your car, you relax, put a smile in your heart and on your face, you avoid creating additional negative energy in the future.

I am not saying you will not have to handle the problem that is there, but you will have stopped yourself from creating a new problem. Learn to focus on the present time and be aware of your environment.

> *You are constantly*
> *being sent signs from the Universe*
> *about what path to take.*

Your soul and the Universe are always sending you guidance. You can learn to read and interpret these messages to help you make the decisions you need to make. Part of sensing energy is learning to hear the messages all around you and to know which to pay attention to and which to ignore.

There are telepathic messages in your relationships with your friends and loved ones, coworkers, bosses, or employees. There are many ways in which you can be aware of their energy while paying attention to your own inner guidance and messages rather than the messages coming to you from others.

Your thoughts are the doorway to sensing energy, and your inner eyes guide you in changing and working with it. You can learn how to transform negative energy. You can evolve your ability to visualize. You can have telepathic communication with people, knowing what kind of energy they are sending you, and choosing to receive or not receive this energy. To do this, you will be working with your inner images, feelings, and senses.

Each of you has a different way of sensing energy. Some of you sense energy as feelings or thoughts; some of you sense energy as wave patterns or colors, or through an inner sense or feeling about it. Some of you are not aware until afterward that you sensed and worked with energy. To sense energy accurately, learn to get quiet, to step outside your thoughts, feelings, and emotions, and to become a blank screen so that you can receive impressions.

Learn to know who you are. Just as you can pay attention to the sounds in a room and nothing else, so can you pay attention to the telepathic and unseen energy that is also there. First, you will want to find out how your inner eyes work. When you hold an object, do you sense a feeling, color, word, thought, or image? Each of you uses a different method; learn to recognize your own way of sensing energy. Some of you sense energy by becoming emotional, some by creating mental images, thoughts, and pictures. Discover this week how you sense energy. You may be reacting to the energy you sense without any conscious awareness of it. You can learn to become more consciously aware of it.

All of you have the ability to stay balanced and centered whenever you notice negative energy. As you do, you can help people evolve, increase the positive energy in your home, and change the nature of your personal relationships. You need not be affected by other people's bad moods, be they mechanics or clerks, coworkers or supervisors, friends or loved ones. If you are a clerk, mechanic, or supervisor, you can learn how not to be affected by the moods or behavior of the people you connect with all day.

People can bring you down and make your life harder — or provide you an opportunity to learn how to work with your own energy to lift yourself higher. This week, whenever you go into a place and you notice you do not like the way you feel there, stop! Become a blank screen and relax. Think of how you want to feel, and begin to visualize yourself as feeling that way.

PLAYSHEET

Chapter 2

Sensing Energy

1. Sit quietly, clear your mind, and imagine a blank screen. Think of a rose. How do you picture it? Can you imagine touching, smelling, or tasting it?

2. Think of the home you live in and the objects in your home. What kinds of thoughts do you have about these? Send your home and the objects in it thoughts of how much you love them. Fill your home with light, joy, and loving thoughts.

3. Practice relaxing. Take a deep breath and picture warmth and lightness spreading throughout your body. Mentally go through your body and observe any areas of tension. Let those areas relax. Practice relaxing yourself at least two more times today. See if you can become more aware of your body when it tenses up, and then consciously create relaxation.

Understanding and Directing the Unseen Energy around You

Energy exists all around you. It exists as the thoughts and feelings that people around you project. Energy comes from the earth itself; plants, trees, and animals all emit energy. Each place on earth has a different energy, each neighborhood, each community. High altitudes have different energy than low altitudes; cities have different energy than small towns. Everything is alive in your world and emits energy, which you can learn to sense.

You are a magnificent energy-sensing being. You can sense energy in many ways, with touch, sight, hearing, smell, feelings, thoughts, and physical sensations. You can sense the world in ways that will give you much valuable information, tuning in to people's energy on a physical, emotional, or mental level by simply practicing.

You can learn to tune in to anyone, physically present or not. You can pick up people's thought images, their inner beliefs, and even their cries for help. Be aware that you cannot violate people's privacy in areas that they or their souls do not wish to reveal, because the soul is able to veil from anyone what it does not want to expose.

You can become aware of other people's thoughts and emotions, and even of future events, to a degree you never dreamed possible, if you want to do so. To sense what is going on around you in a way that allows you to interpret and use the information, you need certain attitudes and skills, all of which you can learn easily if you are willing to pay attention and practice.

The more you can become aware
of other people's energy,
the more aware you can become
of your own inner guidance.

The more you can sense energy, the more you can hear your inner guidance and your higher wisdom. The next step is to become aware of what other people are sending you and how it is affecting you, and to also recognize how your energy is affecting others.

You are constantly sending thoughts and pictures to other people. It is important to become consciously aware of the images you are sending them if you want to create with awareness the reality you live in. You can send positive images to yourself with your imagination, and help others by sending them positive images as well.

The first skill to develop for sensing energy is the ability to pay attention. Learn how to observe others by being silent. You know what it is like to sit back and watch. Observe any area about which you want more information, without judgment or having any opinions or preconceived ideas about it. As you think intently about something, you will begin to receive guidance, ideas, and new thoughts about the issue.

After you stop and pay attention, the next step is to assume an attitude of confidence and trust the information you are receiving. When you first begin sensing energy by tuning in to your future, or in to other people, you may doubt what you are receiving and wonder if you are making it up. Doubts can be a friend if they keep pushing you to be more accurate and precise in what you sense, as long as doubts do not stop you from continuing. Begin by believing in what you are sensing.

As you sit quietly and ask to see what lies ahead for you in a certain area of your life, thinking of a decision you want to make or a path you want more information about, bits and pieces of information should begin coming to you. Your intent to know the future sends your mind out to that future time, and it will bring data back to you. Sometimes information comes as a vague feeling, such as a feeling of joy or discomfort. Do not hold expectations of what you will experience. It is also important not to judge your initial attempts but to let any impressions come in.

A writer who is opening the flow of creativity must temporarily suspend judgment. Any creative person must suspend his or her judgmental, critical part during the time new information is coming through. Later, this part will be valuable in refining the information, but initially it is better to remain open.

Likewise, when you first begin to receive impressions, suspend your judgment. Do not be critical, asking, "Is this right, or is this wrong? Am I just making this up?" for that will stop the impressions from coming in. Let the impressions continue to flow. You may even want to jot them down, for you will discover later that what seems obvious and simple as it comes through often seems profound later on. When you do not write down impressions, you often forget them. When you record your impressions, you will get feedback when you read them later.

Feedback is a very important part of your reality. In your world, actions create reactions, and it is important to be able to observe what reactions your actions cause. If you have been tuning in to energy and you are beginning to get data, feelings, and thoughts back, record them. Several months from now, you will probably be amazed to see the way these impressions connect with your decisions and what actually happens. It is a good way to open your awareness.

*You can sense energy
to the degree your heart
is open and loving.*

As you tune in to others, open your heart and embrace them with a thought of love, not criticism. Imagine an unloving, critical person tuning in to someone's energy. The other person would not open (even subconsciously or at an energy level) to reveal any information, for that critical energy would feel like an intrusion. Then imagine a gentle, caring, and loving soul seeking information. The other person would open to that warmth and bask in that love.

As you start to sense energy, you will discover not only the pain and confusion in others but also different reality systems that may not fit into your own. If you approach people with compassion and tolerance, you will be able to gather much more useful information.

Many people are very aware of energy, and yet when they sense something that does not fit with their known reality, with life the way they believe it to be, they tune it out. To accurately perceive people's energy, you will need to accept that many people think and feel differently than you do, without making their opinions or beliefs wrong or less than yours.

Tolerance means you can accept many different viewpoints and love people for who they are. If you are willing to be tolerant, you can embark on an enormous adventure. Each person has a unique way of looking at the world.

If you can discover what is unique, free, open, and loving about everyone you know and meet, you will discover new ways that you yourself may become more free, open, and loving. It is fascinating to discover the ways people perceive the world. As you open to many beliefs, you yourself will become more fluid and less rigid.

To grow lighter, be flexible and adopt whatever viewpoints are appropriate to the outcomes you desire. Most people are fixed within their own being. They have been taught the world operates in a certain way, and that is how they see it. This inflexibility leaves them with fewer and fewer areas of freedom and choice. You have seen people who are stuck in certain ruts. They are unwilling to change even though their lives are not working.

These people may be unaware of other people's energy. They see everything in the world, not as they affect it, but as it affects them. They look at the world as if it revolves around them. Because they view the world this way, they often feel powerless to change things to achieve the results they want. Because they assume they are the center of the world, they are usually unaware of other people's feelings and what reactions and consequences they are creating by their actions and deeds.

If you want to direct the energy in your life, if you want to see clearly the world you live in, you will need to be willing to see life from other people's perspectives, which may be quite different from your own. As you do so, remain open and nonjudgmental, keeping a sense of discovery, love, and adventure.

Your imagination provides a powerful way to sense energy.

Another faculty you can use to sense energy is your imagination. You have been given an imagination to picture and then create things that do not yet exist in physical reality. Unbounded by belief structures, your imagination is one of your most powerful energy-sensing faculties.

As you use your imagination in positive, uplifting ways, so do you connect with higher and finer energies. Imagination is not bound by time and space; it is not bound by your physical body. When you make things up, you often do it with a sense of joy and play, in a state of relaxation. This is a highly intuitive state.

Imagination can also be used to create fear, such as when you imagine yourself or a loved one being hurt, worry about losing a job, or are afraid of catching someone's illness. It is better to use your imagination to pretend that you know what action to take, create pictures of people loving you, or imagine yourself healthy and well. When you choose to express the lighter energy of playfulness, when there is less worry, fear, or anxiety surrounding the outcome, you are often more accurate in what you sense.

If you want to sense energy, sit quietly and pretend that you can do so. If you do not know how to do something, pretend that you do, for the subconscious does not know the difference between pretending and what is truly happening. The subconscious accepts whatever you pretend is real and will use it to create your outer reality. I tell people to "magnetize your goal to you," and they tell me they do not know how. I tell them to pretend they know how — and it works!

As you sit, pretend that you know what someone is thinking or feeling. Put yourself in that person's shoes, and imagine what his or her life might be like. Imagine that you do know which decision you are going to make. Use your abilities to draw in creative ideas and to imagine possible outcomes as a way to sense energy and choose those paths and decisions that create your highest future.

Focusing speeds up time and directs energy.

Focusing is like having a laser beam compared to an overhead light. To sense energy, use your ability to focus. Focus is the ability to concentrate on one idea to the exclusion of all others. If you want to find information, it is important to focus upon it.

The degree of focus you put on it will determine how fast you gain the knowledge you seek. Focus takes you directly to what you seek. As you concentrate on something, thinking of it to the exclusion of all else, you are directing your mind like a laser beam. When your mind is directed in this way, you cannot be affected by other energies in the world; you are protected in that sense, and what you focus on becomes clear.

Imagine that focus is like a beam of energy that goes out into the future, into another person, or into whatever you want answers about, and lights up that area. It is like a beam of energy that goes out from you and sets up a way for energy and knowledge to come back. If there is anything you want to become aware of, focus upon it.

As you become aware of energy, you will want to determine whether it is energizing or draining you. You have the ability to determine that by monitoring your energy. If you are paying attention to a certain situation and feeling drained, acknowledge your ability to know and sense truth. If you are involved in any situation, you know if it is draining or energizing you. Become even more aware of those things that energize you, for whatever you put your attention on attracts more of the same.

If you are in a difficult situation,
radiate love.
Love heals and protects you.

Notice that the situations, people, or thoughts that energize you are those that operate in a positive framework, those that encourage your growth and expand your heart. Life seeks energy, awareness, and love. Every situation teaches you more about who you are.

If you find yourself in a difficult situation, one that is causing you trouble or draining your energy, ask to feel the love of your higher self, and let it pour into you. The radiance of love will assist you in not feeling drained. As love goes out, it protects the sender and stops any drain of energy.

Before you sense energy, balance and center yourself. This means putting your body in a relaxed, calm state and quieting your emotions. Grow very silent within and let go of any preconceived ideas or pictures. To sense energy, you will need to learn self-monitoring techniques. As you send out your mind to other people to sense their energy, notice if your pulse rate increases, if you feel tense, or if your body changes in some way. All of these can be ways in which you sense energy.

As you tune in to another person, notice what is on your mind, for the more closely you can monitor yourself, the more data and information you can gather. If you are thinking of someone and you find yourself suddenly worried about your finances, and you were not worrying about finances before you thought of him or her, then you are picking up the other person's worry.

If you are trying to look into the future to see the outcome of something, often the information will come back not through your mind but through your body. You may be trying to decide upon a path, and as you think of one choice you notice that your breathing has grown shallow, your body is somewhat closed, and you feel discomfort in your stomach. These are signs from the future you are sensing that are telling you about this path.

If, when you think of a certain path, you feel heavy inside, your body is telling you there is a better choice to make or a higher way to do things. Keep imagining possible futures, varying slightly the things you are thinking about doing, until you have a light and joyful feeling. If none of them gives you a light feeling, try out some new alternatives. Learn to monitor yourself, for doing this allows you to sense energy, and as you monitor yourself you begin to find the clues and answers that are there.

Interpreting what you have received is the next step. After you have brought all the information in, even recorded it, sit and read it or review it in your mind. You may find many doubts coming up; it is important at this time that you do not let them stop you. Thank them and let them go. As you expand your abilities to read the energy around you, you may discover that there is a voice within that does not believe what you are sensing. It is true for almost everyone, so do not fault yourself if you discover this to be so.

As long as your heart is open, as long as you are not coming from ego, personal gain, manipulation, or any energies you know are not high, you can trust what you are sensing. Sometimes the information you gather may seem to serve the ego. If it does, you must examine it closely, using both your mind and your ability to sense energy. If it is something you have wanted to happen, and you are emotionally very involved in having it happen, then your ability to sense clearly may be impaired.

The clearest information comes when the emotions are calm, when there is no personal gain, and when you are simply seeking information to assist another. As you practice, however, you can still bring in valuable information about yourself even when you are feeling emotional about an issue.

Perhaps you have a friend who is in trouble. You sit quietly one day, using all of the techniques I have mentioned, sensing your friend's energy. You begin to see life through his or her eyes. You see that there are certain beliefs that are not working for this person and that there is pain inside. You see this without judgment, with only a sense of love and compassion. As you sense this friend's energy, there is no personal gain for you or sense of manipulation; there is only a true desire to help. Trust the information that comes in.

Ask for your higher self to be with you and for the higher forces of the Universe to assist you. Request that you become a channel for higher information, and be open to any information that you receive. If your intent is to create more light in your life and others' lives, then what you receive will help you in doing so. If you act in this manner, from the heart, with a sense of service, your ability to sense energy will increase rapidly and doors will open for you.

> *Spend time thinking of what you want rather than what you do not want.*

The less time you spend sending out pictures of what you want, the more your space will be filled with other people's visions of what they want you to do, or with lower or less-evolved images that come from old patterns. You will be living those pictures rather than having what you want. Imagining what you want is like creating a model before you build the real thing. The images direct the energy.

If there is a situation in your life you would like resolved, you can always ask your higher self to send you images and symbols that will help you. Often, when you receive these images and pictures, you want to find logical explanations and know the meaning of them. It is not necessary to know what they mean to be uplifted and helped by them.

You can send people symbols and images to assist them in experiencing higher, more positive states. You can change a situation for the better by envisioning and symbolizing it as easily as you can alter it with words. Symbols are, in fact, more direct and more transformative than words, for they are not connected to any of your belief systems.

Think of a situation in your life right now, something you would like an answer to, and ask for an uplifting, healing image for this situation. See if you can get an image of the other person involved or a sense or feeling of the entire situation.

If you have someone in your life who is causing you trouble, tying up your time and energy, try to see him or her symbolically. This person may appear to be coming at you with a battering ram, and you might imagine yourself as a wall that constantly gives in to that force.

You could work with the situation by changing and healing the symbols, perhaps imagining the battering ram changing into a tiny piece of cardboard and your wall becoming flexible like rubber. Or, you might imagine yourself stepping aside completely, becoming transparent, and letting the other person's energy bypass you completely. You absolutely can shift energy by playing with symbols and inner images, and in this way you can change any situation for the better.

There are currents of energy circling the planet, and you can tap into them anytime you want. If you want physical energy, you can breathe deeply and imagine connecting with the flow of all people who have an abundance of vitality. At any one time there are millions of people focused on certain ideas. There are photographers, writers, meditators, and spiritual people, to name a few, and you can harmonize with their energy, amplifying in yourself whatever energy you want to resonate with. Simply close your eyes and tune in (even if it is just with your imagination) to all those people who are doing the same thing that you are doing or that you want to do.

Tune in and move into harmony with their high, successful energy. Through your intention to do this, you can experience a global connection to other people doing what you want to do or are doing. You can open to the assistance and guidance that are always available, emanating from your higher self and from the higher forces of the Universe.

Any energy you want exists in the world. If you want more love, you can open to the love that is there, circling the planet. Sooner or later it will appear in your physical reality; you may notice that you can more easily express and experience love. If you are working on a project and find difficulties in completing it, you can tune in to all the people out there who are successfully completing their projects. You can be a positive, uplifting influence. Use your ability to sense and tune in to energy to evolve yourself and others; it is a skill you can develop that will help you evolve rapidly.

PLAYSHEET

Chapter 3

Understanding and Directing
the Unseen Energy around You

1. Take one person you know and describe the person's life as
    he or she experiences it. Ask for a symbol or image of this
    person with which you could work.
2. How could you help and support this person in his or her
    growth? Make a picture in your mind of what you could do
    to assist him or her. If you receive a symbol or image with
    which to work, make this image or symbol as beautiful
    as you can imagine it to be. As you do, you are changing
    your thoughts and feelings about this person, changing the
    inner messages you are sending him or her. Doing this will
    assist this person in making his or her life better in some
    way.
3. Take a situation in your life whose future outcome you
    want to know more about. Now pretend that you are five
    years in the future and looking back at today. What does
    your future self have to tell you about what will happen?
    Let your imagination run free and have fun with this. (You
    might want to keep a note about the images or informa-
    tion you received, to look at later.)

Sensing Energy in Others

Many of you are developing the ability to maintain your sense of self and steer clear of the mass or group thinking that does not fit you. Mass consciousness can be thought of as an aroma drifting around, affecting or not affecting you depending upon how you choose to react to it and how aware you are of it. The more aware you are of yourself, the less outside influences can affect you. The less aware you are of yourself and the less attention you consciously pay to who you are, the more energy can affect you.

All of you are aware of your feelings and thoughts to one degree or another. You certainly know when you feel happy or depressed; you know whether your thoughts are negative or positive. You can learn to go deeper, becoming aware of the subtle currents and flows of energy and how they affect you. You can become an observer of the energy around you, flowing with it rather than reacting negatively to it or struggling against it.

For a moment, think back on your day. What feelings did you have today? Can you remember how you felt when you were with various people? You probably experienced many different emotions, ranging from high, happy, positive thoughts and experiences to possible feelings of anger, frustration, anxiety, or depression. Some of your feelings may have been reactions to the people you were with.

People constantly broadcast their energy. Just as people have their own personal body chemistry, so do they have their own unique energy broadcasts. You might equate a personal broadcast to a snowflake. Just as no two snowflakes are alike, no two people or broadcasts are alike. Each person you are with can affect you somewhat differently.

Become aware of your body when you are with a particular person. Are you hunched over, or are you straight? Are your arms folded in front of you, or are your arms in back of you, leaving your heart open? Are your shoulders back or forward? Are you leaning forward or backward from the waist, or are you straight up and down? Your body will always give you clues about how you are handling people.

Awareness of your body,
thoughts, and emotions
allows you to discover the
effect other people
have on you.

Tomorrow, or for the next week, notice how you feel with each person you come in contact with. Pay attention to your emotions. You may not feel as if people are affecting you until you take a deeper look at what is happening to you. When you are with one person, you may suddenly start worrying about finances, although 10 minutes earlier you felt fine about money. In this case you have brought his or her energy into yourself.

If you are leaning forward, you are giving away your energy and trying to push in on other people's space. If you are leaning way back, you are avoiding their energy, and they are coming at you too strongly. When you are sitting or standing straight, with your shoulders square, you are in your power, for this is a position of balance and centeredness that allows you to flow with the energy around you. With both feet flat on the floor, your body breathing rhythmically, and your shoulders square, you are in a good position to act and speak as your higher self.

You can also become more aware of the effect people have on you by paying attention to your thoughts. Note what issues you begin thinking of when you are around various people. When you are with one person, you may find yourself constantly thinking of love, transformation, and the beauty of the Universe. When you are with another, you may find yourself thinking how hard things are, how difficult your life is, how much work you have ahead of you.

Monitor your thinking when you are with people and when you spend time alone. Unless you know how you think when you are alone, you will not be able to recognize the effect other people have on your thoughts.

Look out for the effect others have on your emotions too. You may feel suddenly tired; or happy and charged with energy; or drained, depressed, anxious, or angry. Pay attention to the differences. Learn how to let your connections to people activate and charge you instead of draining you. The first step is to become aware of when someone's presence leaves you drained, even in a very subtle way.

Many of you make yourselves wrong when you feel depleted by people. You say, "I am not trying hard enough to please them." Or, "Maybe I did not say the right thing." "Maybe I did not get my point across." "Maybe I was not good enough or loving enough." You look for ways in which you might have been wrong, and then you step up your efforts to please the other person.

Do not make
the other person, or yourself,
wrong.

You cannot have a healing connection if you hold thoughts or images of yourself as wrong or lacking. If you are feeling bad about a relationship, say to yourself, "I am perfect as I am." Then go deeper into yourself. Monitor your energy when you are speaking to that person. Be aware of your feelings, thoughts, and body. Constantly check in with yourself and ask, "Do I feel good or do I feel inadequate?" There is absolutely no reason to be around anyone who makes you feel bad about yourself.

As you deepen your awareness of the energy dynamics of a situation, you can pick up messages from the interaction that will tell you more about yourself. For instance, suppose you are talking to someone, and it seems that this person only wants to talk about himself or herself and does not want to hear about you. You feel depreciated and angry, or maybe you feel this person does not respect you. As you look into yourself, you may realize that you do not listen to or value your feelings, or that you have many inner messages to which you are not paying attention. As you change the drama within yourself, you will find that you do not attract those types of interactions anymore.

Unless you are involved in healing and know how to work with people who want to drain or use your energy, do not put yourself around them. When you heal people, you direct the energy, and they cannot make you feel depleted. (Unless you take in their energy or they are resisting your healing.) There is no reason to put yourself in a situation where you do not feel appreciated or accepted.

Why do you allow yourself to be in situations throughout the day, with friends or loved ones, or even minor interactions with store clerks, customers, or telephone calls, in which you feel depreciated? You may believe that you do not have the right to choose who you are around. You may feel you owe your time and energy to others, that you are obligated to give them attention if they want to be a part of your life.

You might believe you must be loving, supportive, and caring to everyone no matter how they treat you. Loving someone does not mean making that person's feelings more important than your own. If you study the lives of highly evolved beings, you will discover that there are many ways to offer love to others, including being blunt and not tolerating petty behavior, although high beings usually speak the truth with compassion and love.

Being committed to your higher purpose and loving to yourself is the first priority. In your day-to-day contacts, know that you do not owe anyone your time or energy. They are the greatest gifts you have been given, and how you use them will determine how much you evolve in this lifetime.

When you are feeling
depreciated, angry, or drained,
it is a sign that other people
are not open to your energy.

They may be receiving your energy in a way that is not healing, perhaps to feed their egos. They may be blocking you and not wanting your energy. When you notice that you are feeling depleted in any way, that you are leaning forward, trying to reach others, begging for their attention, or feeling drained, unappreciated, unacknowledged, or unsupported, it is time to ask why you remain in that situation.

When you feel depreciated or drained by a stranger for no apparent reason, you may be suffering from what has been called a "psychic whack." These connections are messages from the Universe telling you to pay attention to what you are doing to yourself, to look at ways you may be giving away your energy to those who cannot receive it. I call them reminders.

The minute you find yourself being whacked or depreciated by someone you will probably not see again, or know only as a distant contact, look more closely at the relationships you have with friends and loved ones. You may be depreciating yourself in some way.

If the Universe cannot reach you with its messages about those close relationships, it will send a stranger to you to catch your attention. It is only a reminder that there is some area in your life in which you are undervaluing yourself. Thank the person for that reminder, and then begin to look more closely at your relationships. Ask, "Where am I giving out my energy and not having it returned?"

Most of you want to support and help the people you know and to have loving and meaningful connections with them. Loving relationships come when the people you love and assist are open to receiving. Imagine you had neighbors you wanted to give to, so you constantly sent them gifts. They, on the other hand, felt irritated and resented the feeling that you were putting them under obligation when they did not have the time or desire to return your gifts. You would begin feeling unappreciated, wondering why they did not thank you or give back to you. You would question why you did not feel good even though you thought that you were being kind and generous to them. As you can recognize, there are many times in which it is not appropriate to give to others. They might begin to resent you because they have not asked for your gifts.

If you want a positive, uplifting connection with others, know how much to give and how much to receive.

It is important to know how much you are capable of receiving, for many of you are not very open to accepting anything, although you love to give to others. If you feel that others do not appreciate what you give them, it is time to take a look at how open you are to receiving from others. All of you have had the experience of not being appreciated. Ask yourself, "Was I trying to give more than the other person was capable of taking in?" That is another way your friends can drain you.

People in the healing professions can feel drained and depreciated, can experience burnout, when their gift of energy is not flowing both ways. There is nothing more energizing to both the healer and the receiver than a two-way flow of love. Then healing can occur. The healer is just as charged by the person receiving energy as the person receiving it is invigorated by the healer. When you are in a healing role with people, you can feel drained if they cannot receive, and they can feel drained if you give more than they can receive.

Negative emotions such as obligation, anger, and resentment always come up when you allow people to drain your energy. If you monitor yourself by checking in on your thoughts, feelings, and body, you will know if the energy exchange is equal.

If you find that you are being depleted, or do not like how you feel, what action can you take? First, know that you absolutely can control your thoughts, emotions, and physical-body reactions. You can go inside and ask the Universe and your higher self to help you sense energy clearly, to speak to you of your lessons.

Many of you are in situations in which you feel the energy exchange is not equal. Suppose someone is constantly borrowing money from you and not paying you back. The more you try to get them to repay you, with no results, the angrier you get. You can go within and ask, "Is this situation symbolic of my giving away my energy and not being open to receive any energy back?"

You can find many messages about how your energy flows by paying attention to those areas in which you feel drained, and you can reframe those messages as challenges and lessons. If you have a belief that says you do not deserve to have all that you want, affirm to yourself that you can have relationships that are fulfilling and rewarding for both you and others.

Most of you have reservations about the energy you sense. You may think, "Am I really sensing this energy, am I really feeling depreciated and drained, or am I just tired today and imagining it?" Do not worry about your doubts. They can also represent your strong side that keeps the various currents of energy around you from pulling you off course.

The key is learning to turn your doubts into friends. Sometimes you will hear a voice of disbelief speaking up about certain things in your life. It says, "Maybe it will never work.

Maybe it is all a pipe dream. Maybe I will never get what I want. Maybe I am not right."

That little voice of uncertainty can be so big. Listen to it and talk to it, for that voice always offers valuable information. What could be the message, the benefit of that voice of doubt? Many of you respond to the voice by saying, "No, I will not be discouraged. I will keep the faith. I will keep my vision. I am going to try anyway." When you encounter the voice of skepticism and do not let it control you, it has already accomplished its goal, which is to bring out your strong side and strengthen you.

Sometimes the doubts can seem almost overwhelming, and your powerful voice must become even louder for you to hear and pay attention to it. When you feel yourself experiencing doubts — questioning your power, your interpretation of things, or your path — talk to that voice expressing doubts and ask it what it is trying to tell you.

Ask what gift of awareness it wants to give you. The sooner you acknowledge and open to the gifts that the voice of uncertainty is offering you, the more quickly the doubts will go away and you will be able to better trust the energy you are sensing in yourself and others.

The other message from the voice of doubt is a challenge to help you discover how much you believe in yourself. When you wonder if you really feel drained or not, your lesson is to believe in your feelings. If you feel even the slightest bit drained, begin to look at the energy dynamics between you and the person you are with, or someone you were with during the day. Trust that you would not feel drained unless you really are, or were, being drained.

Emotions help you create reality.

Emotions can lead you to answers but can also block a clear connection to your intuition when you are sensing energy. What do emotions do, and why do you have them? When you believe in something, when you love, desire, and want it, you can create it more quickly. Love your emotions, but do not let them deplete your energy.

Do not allow the emotions of others to drain you, either. The emotions of other people can exhaust or capture your energy only to the degree to which you allow those same feelings within to capture you. No one can harm you with his or her powerful, intense, or negative emotions, unless you have those same emotions. Other people's feelings awaken within you your matching emotions, through the principle of resonance. As you calm your own emotions, you will be able to handle other people's strong emotions.

How do you calm your emotions? Listen to any slightly negative feelings within you before they create a crisis. Your higher self is always speaking to you through your emotions, leading you this way or that. If you do not listen at the lower level of intensity, your emotions will grow stronger. It is the same when you listen to other people. If you do not pay attention when you are feeling slightly depreciated by people, they may continue to deplete and drain your energy until you "get it." They may exhaust you more and more until you stop them, either by terminating the relationship, or by speaking to them of what you want.

When you begin to notice situations in which people are criticizing you, undervaluing you, or demanding too much from you, clear the negative energy. First, remain straight and strong and centered in your body; do not lean forward or backward. When you are with people who drain you, learn to put your feelings into words, even if just to yourself.

Putting your feelings into words is very powerful and can cleanse other people's energy from your space. Do not express anger to other people, but do get it out of your system. Say it into a recorder or write it down. Any process that brings it out of your internal world and into the light of day is a process of healing and of cleansing yourself of the energy you have taken on from other people.

Emotions can block the clear sensing of energy. When you are highly emotional about an issue, it is much more difficult to be aware of your higher path. Before asking the Universe for answers, be sure to find a peaceful, quiet space within yourself for the answers to flow into.

Many of you, when you listen to others, are constantly chattering in your mind, thinking of answers you will give, of things to say back. I call it doing rather than being. Doing is when your mind is constantly busy carrying on an inner dialogue. Being is when you are inwardly still and focused on listening.

Listen with a silent mind
to stay more centered and balanced
around people.

The busier your mind is, the more you are apt to be unconsciously affected by energy. The quieter your inner dialogue when you are listening to another, the more you can be aware of your body and emotions in the interaction, which helps you monitor how you are being affected by other people's energy.

Doing this opens the door to more compassion, wisdom, and understanding in knowing how to respond to another in ways that lift and empower both of you.

When you are with others, practice trying not to do anything, think of anything, or respond to anything. Simply become aware of the sounds, the smells, the room, and the energy interaction at a level beyond words. Monitor how you feel, and observe what people are saying. You will find a wealth of information flowing into you.

You may be surprised, as you become more aware of the kind of relationships you have been having, that the connections you thought were high and loving were not. You may, for the first time, become truly aware of the energy others are giving or not giving to you. You may also be surprised at how much better your relationships can be when you listen to and become more aware of others.

Be aware of the world you exist in. Be aware of the messages constantly being sent to you by the loving, higher forces of the Universe, and most of all, pay attention to yourself.

PLAYSHEET

Chapter 4

Sensing Energy in Others

1. Sit quietly and relax your body. Tune in to your own energy, your body, emotions, and mind to get a sense of your reality. Then, think of someone you know. Send your mind out gently, open your heart, and listen quietly while any images, pictures, or feelings come back. Notice the difference between your feelings and theirs. Notice any changes in your body or emotions or thoughts, and then come back into your own reality. Record or note any impressions you received.

2. If you choose, share your experience with this person, giving him or her any positive information or loving insights you received. Get feedback, for through feedback you become able to more and more accurately interpret what you receive.

Who Am I?

The question "Who am I?" is important, for without knowing who you are, you cannot clearly sense or interpret the energy around you.

All of you have a sense of who you are; you have observed yourselves in many different situations, and you know how you react, how you use your time, and so on. Most of you also have a vision of who you wish you were — how you would like your body to look, how you would like to spend your time, how much money you want to make, what exercise you should get, and what food you think you should eat. I will speak later of those images and thoughts of who you think you should be, and the vision of who you want to be, that you carry around.

To know who you are, you will need to find the stillness of your mind. I have spoken of stillness and the screen that you can create through relaxation and visualization. Knowing who you are involves time alone, quiet and reflective time in which you can listen to your thoughts and reflect upon the day and yourself.

To know who you are means making a commitment to yourself. What is a commitment to yourself? Some of you think it means using your willpower to force yourself to live that vision of who you think you should be. You may feel that once you have decided to do something, you must stand inflexibly by that decision.

Making a commitment to yourself
means listening to your feelings
and inner guidance
from moment to moment
and acting on what is right
for you in present time.

Almost all of the resolutions you make about how you will act involve projecting your present-time self into a future time. That means making decisions for a time that has not yet arrived. Making a commitment to yourself means being in present time, acknowledging that you have enough sense of self to do what is right in each moment. It means trusting yourself, knowing you do not have to wake up and tell yourself how you will act or think during the day, how you will handle things; you do not have to worry about three weeks from today or a year from now. It means knowing that you will not be the same person at that future time, that you will be wiser and more evolved.

It is important to plan and visualize what you want for the future, if that is what you are being guided to do. Afterward, relax and trust your future self to do what is appropriate at that future time.

Making a commitment to yourself means knowing what is appropriate at the present time. To do so you must know your feelings. You may say, "I know how I feel," yet many of you do not know how you feel, and even more of you do not back your feelings with words or actions.

For instance, if someone asks you to do him or her a favor, you may think, "That is not something I want to do, but I *should* do it." And then you do it, going against your feelings. When you make a pledge to honor yourself, others may call you selfish. You may have programming that says it is wrong to be selfish, that you owe something, or are obligated in some way, to others.

You cannot sense energy clearly, you cannot be powerful and flow with the energy around you, unless your first commitment is to yourself. If you do not make your life, thoughts, goals, and time a priority, you will be lost in the currents of other people's desires and expectations.

Whatever comes your way, such as a person, a project, or an event, will constantly push you back and forth like a small boat on an ocean of huge waves. If you do know who you are, make your life a priority, and acknowledge your feelings and act upon them, you can then be a strong vessel sailing calm waters, in a direction you have chosen.

*K*now when to pay attention to your own needs and when to be selfless.

While it is important to be centered within yourself and know who you are, making your life a priority, it is also important to be aware of your effect on other people. You are more powerful when you understand the effect your actions have on others and then choose what actions you want to take.

Some people worry that if they do what is right for themselves they will be acting in a selfish way. When you honor
your higher path and self, you always honor the higher path
and self of others, even if it does not seem so at the time. It is
also important to know when to be selfless — when to flow
with things and let go of the demands of your ego.

The best guideline I can give is to be selfless when it comes
to the unimportant things — what table you get at a restaurant, what movie you watch. Let small things slide by. When
it comes to following your higher vision, to doing those things
that serve humanity and fulfill your purpose, that is the time
to take a stand.

It is important to be selfless when you are a part of a larger
group working toward community goals, if those goals are
part of your higher purpose and there is a sense of joy in that
service and selflessness. If selflessness comes from guilt, pres-
sure, or a "have to" attitude, then it is not appropriate.

Most of you are wrapped up in your own lives. You are
so concerned with your impact on other people, wondering,
"What will so-and-so think when I tell him or her what I am
doing?" that you often do not know who you are except from
a limited perspective.

There are many ways to change your perspective, to view
yourself in a new light. One is to put yourself in other people's
shoes, to look at them not through your own judgments and
beliefs but through their beliefs and perspectives. You might
feel like an actor on a stage, with everybody watching and
judging you. However, it is only you who has put yourself on
a stage, watching, observing, and judging yourself. When you
do this, you also begin to feel responsible for other people; if
they feel bad, then you may feel you caused it.

*Do not feel responsible
for everyone's happiness.
Only they can choose to be happy;
you cannot choose this for them.*

You have seen small children who feel they caused their parents' divorce, because, in their young eyes, everything that happens appears to be something they caused. If you want to get a new perspective of who you are, see yourself through the eyes of another person.

Put yourself in the other person's shoes. Think of his or her challenges, attitudes, and abundance or lack of it, and let the images flow. You have just left your reality and become a part of another's reality. You will understand another person's actions and behavior by stepping outside of your life and viewpoint, and you will also be able to sense yourself more clearly. Look at your life through his or her eyes.

You can begin tomorrow with some of the people you come in contact with. Use your imagination and think about the reality they are living in, the stress they are under, the kinds of thoughts that go on in their minds, and what their lessons are right now. With this understanding, even though it may seem to be just your imagination, you can interact with them in a way that is healing to you and them.

Make this process a habitual one, something you do without trying or thinking. Then, when you are worried about others, concerned with what they think of you, you will be able to use the same process to sense their energy and point of view. Doing this takes the focus off of yourself and opens your heart. It allows you to feel more compassion and be more understanding about their lives, rather than worry about how they may be judging you.

One of the biggest blind spots in sensing energy is being too aware of yourself, existing too much on the center stage of your own life. You are blocked from sensing other people's realities when you are more concerned with what others think about you than with what you can do to assist them, which, of course, assists you. As I speak of moving upward to higher energy levels, I am speaking of helping others, of making every contact you have throughout the day an uplifting one.

You cannot become more sensitive to energy until you can handle it in an uplifting and supportive way. The Universe would not allow you to experience that much energy if you did not know how to handle it. The more you can work with the energy you sense in a way that uplifts and heals you and others, the more you will be able to sense and know the energies that exist around you.

What is a healing contact? How do you make every connection a healing one? The first step toward creating healing connections is to forgive people as you come in contact with them. First, become aware of any resentment you may have had, or now have, toward them, any feelings of superiority or inferiority, any grudges, any negative thoughts you have sent to them (even if it is only an inner picture you have that implies something about them is not up to your standards). To heal, feel a sense of forgiveness for yourself for anything you have sent them on a thought or emotional level that has not assisted them in their growth.

Ask your higher self how you can assist those people in their spiritual unfoldment. What communication could you give that would serve them? To find an answer, you must listen to your inner guidance. Ask your higher self to assist you in becoming more aware of their realities. Ask for assistance in hearing your inner guidance more clearly. How can you appreciate, acknowledge, and thank them? Those questions and thoughts will take you outside the narrower focus of your personality to experience a higher, wiser understanding of the other person's reality.

> *Give to others what you want to receive — love, support, appreciation, healing, and acknowledgment — and you will get it back.*

Wondering "How can I be acknowledged, have more support, or get what I want?" blocks your clear sensing of other people's energy. Forgiving and releasing judgments opens your ability to become aware of other people's systems of reality, and it most definitely enables you to view yourself in a higher and more loving way. You will automatically begin forgiving, supporting, acknowledging, and appreciating yourself when you forgive, support, acknowledge, and appreciate others. Releasing your judgments about others is not just a gift you are giving to the world. It is also a gift to you.

All of you can learn to be aware of your own energy by becoming aware of other people's energy. The more accurately you perceive energy in other people, the more precisely you will be able to sense it in yourself. This is true not only of positive energy but also of fear and other negative energies.

When you judge others, you feel your own shadow side and bring into yourself any negative energy you are judging. To see or sense energy clearly is to leave behind right/wrong judgments. Challenge yourself to let go of a right/wrong, good/bad framework. When you observe a quality or characteristic in others that you do not like, explore how it fits into their lives. Look at how that particular trait works for them, what that quality does for them. Leaving behind judgment frees you from being affected by other people's energy.

What is fear? What is the shadow side? It is that part of you that may be affecting you through its negative view of the world. You can transform this side with love and by facing your fears. Until you face your fears and see them for what they are, fear can appear as a feeling of distress, anxiety, worry, or concern. There are moments when you feel light and joyful, and moments when you do not. Those worrisome moments are often an indication of fear. The higher and more expanded your consciousness, the more you will release fear.

To dissolve fear,
turn and look directly at it,
for what you face dissolves
in the light of consciousness.

Fear at the lower levels can exist as strong emotions. It can appear as a feeling of tension in the body, mind, or emotions. It can be a feeling of rushing around, trying to hide under the guise of productivity, incessant or obsessive thinking, doing rather than being.

When you feel anxious or gloomy, ask the fear behind this to come into your conscious awareness. Anything you turn your back on will grow and become worse. When you are willing to stand and face what you fear, the Universe will assist you in releasing and healing it.

Many of you fear that you are alone; you believe that you must handle everything yourself. You may feel the great weight of responsibility. Yet the world is full of friends, healers, and help. The more you begin to heal those you contact, the more healing will come back to you. Receiving and giving healing is the pathway into higher energy.

Fear can often be faced and transformed by deep breathing and relaxing. It also can be handled by taking action. When you are sensing negative energy in another, a feeling you do not like, do not run and hide from it. First, suspend your judgment, and then ask the Universe for guidance about what action (if any) you can take. The Universe will always send you assistance when you ask for it. It may come through your thoughts as insights or revelations; it may come through something you see or read; or it may come through something you hear.

When you feel any negativity in another, you can stop it from affecting you by asking how you can offer love and support. You may find that the other person will look for ways to do the same for you. If this person cannot match you in your supportive and loving energy, he or she will leave your life, or you will find yourself creating fewer opportunities to be together.

What is the fear of sensing energy, what is the fear of finding negative energy in others? Is it a fear that they can harm you? Is it a belief that others can bring you down or diminish you? When you become consciously aware of your fear of negative energy, when you are in touch with how you think negative energy can harm you, then you have a basis on which to begin working with it. Only by facing and acknowledging your fear of negative energy can you transmute it into harmless energy. Again, positive, healing energy is always more powerful than negative energy.

You can experience fear in any area where your images of who you are now and who you want to be do not match. Why do you fear who you are not but think you should be? Do you feel disappointed in yourself, that you have let yourself down in some way?

Love and accept who you are, not who you will be or should be.

If you love yourself for who you are, you are living in present time, which is the gateway to personal power. If you love only who you will be, then you are out of your body, living in a future you cannot affect (until it becomes present time and you can act). Look at who you are, compare it to who you want to be, and ask yourself why they do not match. Ask, "Is what I want to be really appropriate to who I am, or is it something I was told I should be?"

The more you can clear yourself of other people's programs, expectations, and pictures of you, the more powerful you will become. Many of those future pictures involve meeting unrealistic or inappropriate standards given to you by others.

Many of those ideals represent beliefs of others that you try to fit onto yourself. Look clearly at your expectations of yourself, especially those you constantly fail to meet. They can be indicators of areas in which who you want to be is not fitting with your true needs. The pain you feel at the difference, the feelings of worry, fear, or distress, exist only because you are trying to "wear" energy that does not belong to you.

Knowing who you are requires reflective time, quiet time. Time alone is some of the most important time you can create.

I am not speaking of time in which you are frantically thinking of something, but peaceful time in which you are not thinking of anything.

The stillness of the mind creates space for ideas to drop into your reality and be born. Inspiration is born in stillness. It may be a week or more before new ideas come into your conscious awareness. However, do not let the time delay keep you from seeing the connection between quiet time and the creativity that comes later.

Being alone, sitting quietly, and allowing yourself to rest physically, emotionally, and mentally will give you an increasingly clear sense of who you truly are, your innermost Self. In those still times you are not playing out any role, so your soul can speak to you more clearly.

You have the clearest sense of your own energy when you are not around others, when you are alone. Some of you are around others all the time, and when you finally find yourself alone you may create a million things to do — anything to keep from being quiet and reflecting on your life. You may have been taught that productivity and creating things you can see, touch, or hear are more valuable than quiet time. However, reflective time is the source of energy revitalization, of clear seeing, of ideas and inspiration.

Begin valuing any time you can set aside to sit or lie down and be quiet. Practice not thinking of anything, for inner stillness allows you to sense energy and become aware of intuitive guidance. It is also one of the highest and most effective forms of self-healing that you can use.

PLAYSHEET

Chapter 5

Who Am I?

1. Think of an upcoming meeting with a friend or loved one.
2. What is the higher purpose of your meeting? It could be to encourage or support each other or to help with a decision. Even if it is purely social, explore whether you can discover the higher purpose in your being together.
3. How could you assist the other person in creating a higher vision of who he or she is? How could this person assist you in the same way? The next time you are together, focus and act on the higher purpose of the meeting.
4. Before you go to bed, let come to mind anyone you could forgive for any perceived "wrong" he or she may have done to you during the day. Forgiveness is one of the greatest gifts you can offer others, and it also frees you, for whatever you give you also receive.
5. After you forgive others, let come to mind anything you did during the day for which you would like others to forgive you. Ask for their forgiveness, and know that doing this clears your energy and lifts up the energy between you and others.

CHAPTER 6

Bringing the Unconscious into Consciousness

You have within you all the tools you need to become what you want. As you learn to sense energy, you can also evolve your experience of the energy you sense. As you become conscious of the energy around you, you can note when your energy is high and bring it even higher. This allows you to evolve the pictures in your mind and focus your intent so that you become clearer, go higher, and expand and evolve.

When you ask the Universe for more, it is important to be open about how it comes, for the Universe will give it to you in the fastest, most efficient way possible. You may need to let go of certain attitudes or images before you can have something, so you will set up situations to release them. If you are ready to go higher, it is time to let go of any pictures about how you will get there.

You can evolve more quickly by bringing your unconscious to consciousness, for the conscious mind is the light that evolves the unconscious. You are by no means run by hidden drives or unknown programs. You have been given the ability to look inward and find answers.

To bring the unconscious to consciousness, focus on finding the light in any situation. You will find answers coming to you without needing to use your mind to analyze and figure things out. If you want an answer, imagine that you hold the situation in your hands. Imagine light coming into that image, and then release it to your higher self.

You are not at the mercy of hidden drives or unknown programs. You have the ability to look inward and find answers.

If you seek an answer, all you need do is ask, then listen. Some things get in the way of your listening, however, and one of those is your picture of what reality is and how it operates. Another interference is a mind that chatters incessantly, one that keeps thinking when you need to rest or think in another way.

Bringing the unconscious into consciousness is the challenge of every situation you are in. If you feel that something you do not understand has happened, already you are spending much time with the intent to solve it, analyze it, and know it. You are sending a beacon of energy out into the world, and immediately answers are being broadcast back to you.

If you expect a certain answer, or for it to come in a certain way, then it will be difficult for new and more expansive answers to come through. Take any question you want answered, and stop thinking of it for a week. Once you have asked a question, it is important to let go of it. If you could take any issue and not think of it for even one day, you would find a whole new energy around the situation.

Another way of bringing the unconscious up into the known is to sit quietly with yourself and work with your images. If you are going back and forth about an issue, then neither answer is completely right. If you had the right answer, you would not be going back and forth. You can help release this situation by picturing yourself finding an answer. Then, be patient and wait until an answer emerges. At some point, once you set your intention to find an answer, an answer will come into your awareness that immediately feels right and motivates you to act.

If you cannot understand why certain things are happening to you, picture yourself understanding things easily and quickly. You can go back into your memory and recall all the times you did understand events as they were happening.

Whatever is happening in your life can come from an image you hold of yourself. The images you send out attract situations to you. These pictures are absolutely available to your conscious awareness. You can change any situation by looking at and changing your vision of yourself.

If you were to put on peaceful music, sit for a few minutes, and think of nothing else except the situation at hand, you might find yourself moving through it very quickly and able to let go of it afterward, not needing to think of it over and over.

Certain qualities help people move into and experience higher levels of consciousness. One is focus. If your mind is always thinking of 10 or 15 issues, it may take weeks to move through them and find resolution. If you find yourself thinking of many things and feeling pressured, scattered, busy, or if you find there is not enough time, then your mind is trying to handle too many things. Each moment has its highest purpose; each person you are with has his or her highest purpose. If you are ready to move into higher levels of energy, you can do so by increasing the amount of time you spend there.

You can become aware, when your energy is down, of what took it there. The things that take most people's energy down include talking about mundane or negative things; reading articles in newspapers or magazines that speak of pain or struggle without a higher reason for it; not listening to the flow of your body (resting when tired, being active when energy is available); thinking of past times in which you were hurt; fearing the future.

You bring up your energy when you do what you feel like doing. If you set a goal to get something done, and yet find you want to do something else, you would raise your energy by getting up and doing the other thing. You may find the goal you set has changed. Or, you may find the break just what you needed to recharge your enthusiasm.

As you focus on
what is good about people,
you enable them to achieve it.

There are many ways to bring up your energy. Start by becoming aware of what you say to people. Are you building them up? Are you holding a high, positive vision of them? Whatever you put your attention on will grow. If you focus on people's weakness, emphasizing in your mind what is wrong with them, you are sending them negative energy that may hold them back. If any situations in your life are not working, the more you picture them as not working, the more you make that your reality. It is the same in relationships: when you hold positive and uplifting thoughts of others, you assist them in living a better life.

When two people first fall in love, they recognize and focus on the best in each other and hold that vision. Suddenly, they find themselves able to accomplish new things and find old, negative patterns leaving. You can greatly assist people by holding an image of their success, joy, and abundance.

Be aware of the images you are creating of yourself when you speak to others.

Do you speak of prosperity, joy, and abundance, or do you speak of pain, problems, and woes? People form images of you as you speak to them. You may think that you would be lying if you were to tell everyone how abundant your life is when it is not. Yet I will say that if you tell everyone how abundant your life is, soon you will be telling the truth! In addition, if you can become aware of and grateful for the abundance you already have, it will increase.

Watch your words and your energy as you move through the day. The instant you notice that your energy is dropping in any way, that doubts are creeping into your mind, that you are feeling bad about who you are, stop. Take a deep breath and look inward for a higher image. You broadcast images from moment to moment, and people pick them up and respond to them.

If you want to know why something happened to you, believe that you do know why. It is important to learn to forgive yourself, because every time you replay a negative memory, making yourself wrong, you are creating it again in the future. In moments of crisis a new self is often born, a baby self, one that has just come into being with the crisis. Like a small child, it may not have the skills to handle things perfectly or beautifully, and yet that self is growing every moment. Sending it images of its wrongness is not a gift to this new self.

> *You never do anything*
> *that is not in some way*
> *an attempt to bring more*
> *light into your life.*

You can go back to any crisis and discover that a new self, a new part of you, was born. It is a stronger and clearer part, a part that is more committed to your life, your truth, your growth.

You may be setting up a crisis right now, a challenge or a dilemma, to prepare for the birth of a new self. You are always going for the light. You may have interpreted what you did as not being the best you could do, so it is important to go back and change your vision, release the memory and forgive yourself, and discover what you learned.

Look at what qualities the situation is developing or has developed in you. It may be leading you to a deeper truth or helping you learn what you want by experiencing what you do not want. You may be learning to become aware of your own light and to become more powerful, assertive, and clearly focused. Whatever you think you are not, you are working on becoming. Whatever you are asking for right now you will have, but it may not come in the way you expect it.

Watch the energy of everyone you meet when they speak to you. Watch their words, and if you sense your energy dropping, become extra alert. Pay attention to the topic. You will find that there are things you can speak of with other people that bring up your energy, and things that do not. You have the ability to change the topic into something that raises the level of the interaction. Notice what thoughts you carry around in your mind. Whatever thoughts are on your mind when you die will be those that will direct you to where you are going afterward. Where are your thoughts during the day? How often are you thinking of your highest vision, your higher self?

*To bring the subconscious
into the higher self,
look at each area of your life and ask,
"What is my highest vision?"*

You may think that you need to be involved in the daily, mundane details of your life, and yet you can take care of these effortlessly if you focus on your highest vision and your higher path. Look at your level of abundance, how much you let the Universe give you. Is there a way to increase how much you receive? It is important to find your deeper motivation. If you want more money, why? What do you think you will get from having money that you do not have now? If you want something, what is your motivation?

Motivation is a driving force that can bring you anything you want. If you knew your motivation, you would know the driving force behind everything you do. You may be saying, "If I had this car, or that job, or a partner, I would be happy." There is more here than meets the eye. If you knew your deepest motivation for having these, you could have your needs met in many ways. It may be that you want more security or delight, to feel more relaxed or loved, or to receive more in general. When you are in touch with the essence of what you desire, you can have it in many ways. If you do not focus on a specific thing to bring you what you want, the Universe can truly begin bringing you abundance in many ways.

When you think of issues you want to resolve, you have two choices — you can ask your higher self to give you a higher vision of the issue, or you can release the issue to your higher self and ask that your higher self take care of it for you. The best solutions come from your higher self.

It is important to create new and higher images of yourself. Ask your friends to hold specific images of you, such as picturing you succeeding at something you are doing. If you do not have new pictures, your mind will be much more tempted to fall back into the old ways of thinking. If you were filled with thoughts of what would be absolutely joyful in your life, such as traveling, more free time, a loving relationship, a physical body that is strong and fit, you would not have time to think at the old, more painful or mundane levels.

When you evolve your images, you evolve the energy you sense. You can control the energy you come in contact with. If you find people talking about you in a way that does not match your higher vision, or thinking about you in a way that is not honoring you, begin broadcasting your own pictures back to them, rather than receiving their negative images of you. If you want them to acknowledge you as strong and powerful, send an image to them of yourself as strong and powerful. If you think of how you are wrong, you will send that image to them and they will find more ways to make you wrong.

*Acknowledge everyone as
expanding and growing,
and you will better recognize
those qualities in yourself.*

Begin broadcasting positive pictures to others. See them as achieving their goals and creating success. Send out high pictures of yourself and others. See the gems that lie buried in people. Acknowledge people when you are with them; speak of their progress, their growth and beauty. If they want to give you a negative story of their life, do not sympathize with them. Instead, be compassionate and help them become aware of the gifts the situation is giving them. If you hear people speaking of negative things, send them positive pictures and change the conversation.

When you receive or become aware of images that show you more about your path, you may question if it is what you are to do or if it is just wishful thinking or incorrect information. You may even wonder if the pictures you get in your mind are the truth or just something you made up. If you hold an image of your higher purpose, then the thoughts and pictures that come into your mind will lead in that direction.

*If you ask for guidance,
trust the messages that come
into your mind.*

Sometimes the guidance you receive may be simple, telling you the next step. It may be something as mundane as going to the post office or writing a letter. Some of you might want to know your path for many months and years ahead, and yet, if you knew it, it would only be a probable form and could perhaps so overwhelm you that you might find it hard to start. You could find it less than joyful to know your whole future in advance, for there is a certain joy in allowing your future to unfold without knowing specifically what is next. If you want more than you have right now, you can have it by trusting.

Once you are determined to have abundance, what will come is even more than you could picture. If you want a vision of what to do with your life and you do not have it, it may simply be a matter of time. You may be getting prepared for that vision. You can bring anything you want to consciousness. If you feel blocked, you can find answers by asking your higher self for them. You can evolve any situation with an image of light, and you can release any problem to your higher self and the Universe to resolve for you in the highest possible way.

Sometimes the greatest sense of joy can come from knowing you are not alone, that if you ask for guidance and assistance it will be there. If you are ready to link up with the Universe, you can have anything you want. You are not alone; if you are centered on your highest purpose, you will find every door opening. The Universe will give you ideas and assistance; people will reach out to you with help, money, advice, love, and support. Make the commitment. Do it now! Go for your highest purpose. Hold steady that vision of your highest good and be open for surprises.

All of you have pictures of what it would mean to love yourself more. For some of you this might mean a better job or the resolution of a problem. If you want more self-love, the first challenge is to discover whether you can evolve your pictures of self-love. You may already be implementing everything you thought of as being loving to yourself several years ago. Yet you may still not feel that you are loving to yourself.

Look at what you want right now and ask, "What is the essence behind it?" If you want, for instance, a new place to live, what is the essence behind it? What do you really want? It may be peace and quiet or more sunlight. You can get all of those things in different ways, right now.

Every time you think of the future, you project energy into it, even if you mumble, "I never get things done," or "I do not know why this happened to me," or "I wish I had not done it." Every comment you make is directing energy toward the past, the present, or the future. If you could become aware of even one-hundredth of the thoughts you are sending out into the future and evolve them, within a month you would know delight that exceeds all of your pictures today.

Every single statement you make about yourself, to others and to yourself, becomes a truth. You project energy every moment. If you want a better future, speak of it, picture it, and talk about it to others. Only you can create for yourself what you want. It is one of the greatest gifts you have ever been given.

PLAYSHEET

Chapter 6

Bringing the Unconscious into Consciousness

1. Think of a situation in your life you would like to understand, perhaps to learn why you created it or what it is teaching you.
2. Sit quietly, relax, and close your eyes. Imagine you are holding the situation in your hands. Imagine light pouring into this situation, and release it to your higher self. See yourself receiving answers. Think of nothing else but this situation for five or ten minutes.
3. In what way is this situation going to add to your personal power as you move through it? What is it teaching you? What soul qualities are you developing (such as love, patience, tolerance, and trust)? As you grow to understand this situation and all the gifts it is offering you, you can move through it more rapidly.

Evolving Your Inner Images: Releasing the True Self

You carry many images of who you are that sit in a matrix of energy around you. What are images? They are pictures of reality you hold in your mind. You use them as models to judge whether or not you are good or bad, to decide how you will act and speak, and to choose who you will be with. They also create your boundaries and limits and determine how far you can go. A lifetime is a journey out of darkness into light; through evolving your images, you can bring more light into your life.

All of you have basic definitions of who you are that you live by. You may view yourself as being strong, hardworking, intelligent, fun-loving, generous, kind, and friendly. You create your experience of reality based on your image of yourself as a man or a woman. Your particular images determine your limits. If you view yourself as generous, for instance, you will either have to be generous all the time or judge yourself harshly when you are not generous.

*Your definition of yourself
as a man or a woman
greatly influences your behavior.*

Group images of women tend to involve serving, taking care of others, being responsible for relationships, being nice, and being liked. Images of men often focus on being assertive and strong and ignoring feelings.

Many viewpoints of reality come from religious upbringing. For a moment, pause and look within. Go back to your childhood and ask what images of the nature of the Universe you carry within you that come from your religious upbringing. You may think there is a God who punishes you when you are bad and rewards you when you are good. You may be afraid of your shadow side.

You might think you have no religion, yet everyone has a religious orientation, even if it is the belief in intuition and your creative self or a belief that there is no higher power. Religious or philosophical beliefs are among the strongest images people have; they determine what you think about the nature of the Universe and how you respond to it. Do you imagine you will be rewarded if you are good? Do you think that certain types of behavior are good and others are not? Those ideas often come from your religious background.

Your parents passed many of their images on to you. You selected your parents for the images they would give you that would bring to consciousness the inner and outer self you chose to work on in this lifetime. Think of your parents for a moment. Who are they? Think of some of their beliefs about money and abundance. Do you have feelings about those beliefs, either good or bad?

Think about how your parents feel or felt about their relationship to each other. Take the parent who is the same sex as you. What does he or she believe about being a man or a woman? Do you share those images? Think about your parent of the opposite sex. What images does he or she have? Do you observe in yourself any of those same relationship patterns?

Imagine that you are standing in the center of a circle and around you are all the people you are close to. Each friend holds a vision of who you are. As you stand in this circle, allow yourself to bring to consciousness the images you are receiving from your friends. Pretend you are facing someone you are very close to — a husband, a wife, a friend, or a loved one. Who is this person? What pictures is he or she sending to you about who you are?

What images are you sending to this person? As you think of what you are sending, ask this person's soul if there are images you could send that would help this person evolve. You can help people grow by focusing on their potential. What pictures of you would you like this person to hold? Recognize and inwardly thank this person for all the times he or she has sent you those positive images, and for the ones he or she is sending you now. Affirm that you will hold a high image of this person as well.

*Pay attention to the pictures
you send people. Are you
holding them back, or
helping them rise higher,
with your images?*

People absolutely pick up the images you hold of them. Often, long-term relationships cannot survive because people are not willing to change their pictures of each other. One may hold on to an old image of the other as immature and irresponsible long after the other wants to change that behavior. Because of that image, it may be harder for the other to change.

All of you have experienced yourself around your parents, who may hold very old images of you that they need to update. Sometimes you go to them with your newfound strength, grown up and mature, and you find that within five minutes you are acting out old, immature roles. Rather than feeling unhappy with yourself, use the opportunity to look at the images your parents hold of you, and realize how affected you can be by other people's views of who you are.

The minute you become aware of other people's pictures of you, telepathically send them a higher image. Often you accept their pictures without question, and not only accept them but act them out. When you do so, you are living other people's scripts for you, rather than writing your own. You are dancing on their stage. As long as you do this, people who do not hold high thoughts about you will be detrimental to be around. However, once you learn to recognize their images, you can begin to change them by sending them new pictures of yourself. Then you can be around them without feeling affected by their images, if you choose to be around them.

One way to free yourself from the grip of a rigid inner image is to exaggerate it in your mind. Say you are criticizing yourself for acting like a child around your parents or otherwise falling into old behavior. Rather than resisting acting this way around your parents, exaggerate it in your mind. Really get into acting like a child. This enables you to notice more easily what those images are. As you exaggerate your images, you stop running from and fearing them, and they cease to control you. Often as you exaggerate behavior, it triggers your humorous side, which can free you from the grip of that behavior.

You can change or eliminate obsessive thoughts and pictures you may flash over and over in your mind. Sometimes they are pictures of pain, or memories of a time when someone abandoned or hurt you, or of a time when you did not get what you wanted. Many people experience a constant flow of negative pictures. Some of it comes from society's images of scarcity, from ideas that there is not enough, that you must work hard and struggle to get what you want, or that someone else's success takes away from yours. People who are learning about spiritual transformation, higher consciousness, and love are broadcasting new, higher, lighter images to the world, including pictures of abundance.

Pictures are easier for people to pick up than words.

As a spiritual teacher, I am constantly broadcasting energy and transmitting images of love and peace. If you would like someone to change, send him or her images. For instance, say you want a person to be more productive. Rather than criticize (which sends a negative picture and reinforces the very behavior you would like to change), imagine the person being productive.

Rather than point out the person's lack of accomplishments, acknowledge and praise each instance when he or she demonstrates the productivity you would like to experience more of. You will be assisting him or her with your picture. And whether or not the person changes, you will find the energy between you lighter.

Your emotions are often less developed than your mind. Society teaches you to value your mind and intellect more than your emotions. There is much more attention paid to educating people's logical minds to think and memorize than to teaching people how to think in ways that uplift them. It is important to evolve your mind and mental pictures, for your thoughts can trigger strong emotional responses. How free are you from the grip of your emotions?

When you find yourself flashing a fearful picture in your mind over and over, and then feeling anger, pain, or fear, it is simply a cry from your emotions for attention and help and, most of all, for love. For instance, if you are feeling exceptionally anxious, and you are constantly flashing pictures in your mind of a situation that brings up anxious feelings, there is a part of you that is crying out for help and love.

Your higher self, your soul, is integrating all the parts of you and bringing them to a higher consciousness. Images that are obsessively painful are a cry from the part of you that longs to feel nurtured and loved. If you catch that part showing you negative pictures, convert those pictures into symbols or images, and work with those symbols or images to make them look more beautiful in some way. Ask your higher self to help you feel better.

Everyone has a side that does not want to be light, joyful, or high in its images or thoughts. Take that side and imagine you are exposing it to the sunlight, letting it breathe fresh air; visualize light coming into your negative or gloomy side. Imagine embracing and loving that part that feels anxious. Within hours you can feel less negative. Every time you do not allow this side to take over, you strengthen your will and increase your connection to your higher self.

Beliefs such as "I am a good person," "I am a spiritual person," "I am a loving person" both determine your behavior and can limit you. If you define yourself with a fixed image, such as "I am a nice person," you will constantly be judging what you do as nice or not nice. If *nice* is defined rigidly for you, such as "nice people always say thank you," and someone you like does not say it, you will have to either change your definition of *nice* or judge your friend as not nice. An inflexible image will trap you in the world of polarities, right versus wrong, good versus bad.

Expand your definitions of who you and other people are. Examine and unlock your images; let them become flexible and open rather than judgmental and closed. As long as you are comparing all your actions to fixed images of how you should be, you will be caught in the world of judgment and unable to evolve to higher levels.

To release images, become consciously aware of them. Honor your conscious mind. The time you spend analyzing yourself, while in a peaceful state, brings your unconscious into consciousness; and through this process evolution occurs. Every time you find a negative or limiting self-image, imagine light coming into it. You need not do anything else. (If you want to put more energy into it, you can find a symbol and play with it, evolving the symbol and making it more beautiful in some way.) Simply imagining light coming into the picture will change it for the better. Use your imagination consciously.

What do you want? You may spend a great deal of time thinking of what you do not want, perhaps filling your mind and spirit with pictures of injuries or wrongs that others did to you. Every time you flash those pictures in your mind, you are literally sending them out to the future and creating them again.

Negative things happen to you only to show you an image you are carrying that is not aligned with your higher good. Thank anything to which you respond negatively, anything you label as a problem, for bringing your attention to a part of you that needs healing, growth, and more light.

Use your imagination to picture
the highest spiritual path you can take,
to create a vision of why you are here.

Ask yourself, "What is the most spiritual thing I can do with my life?" Beyond the forms you create, what is your highest aim? What is the most important thing you want to do? It may be that you want to evolve into your soul's consciousness. You want to grow spiritually as fast as you can comfortably handle, be a healer, or fulfill your higher purpose. Hold that vision every day.

Go as high as you can with your imagination. Fantasize about your perfect life. The higher you go, the more you connect with your higher self, the more quickly the images and thought forms that do not fit your growth will dissolve.

Do not reach ahead just a year or two but also ask, "What could be my greatest accomplishment during this lifetime?" Do not worry about the form or how you will do it. Every time you create one picture or vision, you open the door to an even greater picture. Hold an image in front of you. Let the energy of that image come into your body. Become consciously aware of the light in everything you do, and you will evolve rapidly in this lifetime.

Know that other people will reflect back to you every image you carry within. If they say something negative to you and evoke a strong response, thank them for reflecting back to you an image of yourself you need to change.

When you carry images such as "I am powerful; I truly love and value myself; I have enough money, enough love," and so forth, you will begin to experience other people sending those images back to you. Consciously send others higher images. Hold a vision of your higher self in everything you do. Honor the higher self in everyone you meet, and you will find it honored in you.

PLAYSHEET

Chapter 7

Evolving Your Inner Images:
Releasing the True Self

1. Write out or mentally come up with a description of yourself in as many words as you like. For instance, "I am a spiritual person."

2. Now expand this description, make it an even higher or more complete picture of who you are. Speak of yourself in the most complimentary, glowing terms you can, being truthful, of course. For instance, "I am a hardworking, loving person who cares deeply for other people. I make my spiritual growth a priority. I practice unconditional love as often as I can." Make this description as high and loving as you can.

3. Notice how you felt as you came up with the second description. The more often you can view yourself from a higher perspective, the more accurately you are seeing who you are.

4. Realize that any image of yourself can be a limit; now release any images you hold of yourself, and open to the freedom to be who you are in each moment, free from all self-definitions and labels.

CHAPTER 8

Finding Your Deepest Truth

This lifetime is a journey of finding your deepest truth. Every situation in your life that is a source of struggle or pain is an area in which you are learning about being true to your soul, your innermost Self.

You have many roles you play, and you experience different truths at different times. You may rehearse a speech, but when you meet someone, you find yourself saying something completely different. So you ask, "What is truth?" What is true one moment may not be true the next. Is truth fluid or is there a deeper truth that will last from moment to moment? All of you are fluid at the personality level, with many identities. Your soul, your core self, holds that deeper truth that is unchanging and constant.

Compassion is the
ability to put yourself
in the other person's shoes.

Finding truth means living from your heart and moving closer to your soul. Finding truth means holding every situation up to the light. What is that light? It comes foremost from the heart and is a deep level of compassion.

In developing the quality of compassion, you will be developing the ability to know and express your deeper truth. All of you have experienced being with people who caused you pain by not honoring or valuing you. You may have wanted something from them that you were not getting. You can always handle the situation by approaching it from a deeper level of compassion.

You may ask, "What is the benefit of expressing my deepest truth?" When you live and express your truth with love and kindness it brings the joy, peace, and serenity that so many of you desire.

Truth also comes from the feeling level. How many times have you had a feeling to call somebody and found that he or she was thinking of you when you did, and it was the perfect time to reach that person? How many times have you had a feeling that it was not the time to call someone, but you ignored it and called anyway, and found the energy did not work between the two of you or the person was not available?

Every one of you has the ability to fine-tune your capacity to sense energy and know truth. How do you find this deeper inner truth? How do you step outside of all the images you live by and the roles you play?

*You do not have to go through
pain and struggle to grow.*

The doorway to deeper truth is awareness. It is paying attention to, and holding up, the vision of truth. The more you act from your integrity, the more evolved you become. Every situation in your life that requires truth from you, that requires you to reach into a deeper level of your being, is an opportunity to grow. The more pain and struggle you experience, the greater the amount of energy you clean up when you live from a deeper level of truth.

Thank those situations in your life that seem difficult or painful. Know that they are opportunities to reach a deeper truth. Not a truth that will separate you, bring you anger, justify your feelings of separation, or make the other person wrong and you right or vice versa, but a truth that will allow you to connect at a deeper level.

To raise your energy higher, go inward and ask if you are withholding from yourself the truth of what you feel or think about the other person. If you do not let yourself recognize the truth, you will have another person and another sent your way until you do get in touch with your deepest truth.

For instance, you may have always wanted affection and nurturing from your partner. You get into relationships that do not satisfy these deeper needs, and you tell yourself you should not, and do not, need to have your needs fulfilled. Your deepest truth is that you do need this, and until you get in touch with that truth and act upon it you will continue to experience pain.

Every time you act and speak the truth with integrity, you lighten your energy. Your past beliefs, lesser thoughts, and stuck emotions can appear as a fog around you that stands between you and the light of your soul. Each time you speak and connect with the light of truth, the energy around you becomes finer and lighter, until the fog is dissipated and the light of your soul pours into you and radiates through you and out to the world.

Every drama in your outer life is a reflection of a drama in your inner life. Every person you are interacting with in your outer life symbolizes an interaction of energy that is going on within you. Think of a person in your life you are struggling with. Imagine you are looking at yourself through his or her eyes. Put yourself in his or her place. Go into your heart and imagine coming from a deep, compassionate level of truth when you are with this person.

For example, if you have been feeling angry with or resentful of someone, and you open up to experience your deepest truth, you may realize that you really do love this person even if he or she disappointed you. From that place within you, you can let go of the hurt and speak to this person with love. Picture this person responding with joy as the energy between you grows lighter.

Every person and event offers you an opportunity to evolve yourself and move into a higher consciousness. The greatest reward is that once you clear up an issue, you will usually never have to deal with it again. Another person cannot hurt you unless you are hurting yourself. You cannot be betrayed, undervalued, or unloved unless you are doing it to yourself by not valuing and loving yourself.

*You have the greatest power of all,
the ability to heal and evolve yourself.*

When you change, heal, and evolve yourself, everything around you that represented your inner struggle dissolves. You can heal yourself by speaking the truth from a deep level of compassion. For instance, you may be thinking that someone does not value your feelings. As you look one level deeper at the truth, you say to yourself, "She is just being herself, and she is not very aware of anyone's feelings — not just mine." Or, "He is in pain himself and does not realize he is hurting me." As you look even deeper, you realize that you have let people treat you that way, that you have not valued your own feelings, and that there have been many times you wanted to speak up. You can continue to look deeper until you feel a release from the pain and acceptance for the person involved.

Look at the different personalities within you. One is very strong, another observes everything you do with detachment, another is young and emotional, and another is very wise. If there is any drama going on around you, you can know that there is a drama going on inside of you between your various parts.

One woman felt betrayed by her girlfriend when a secret she had confided was told to another. Upon closer examination, she realized that she had betrayed her true Self in many ways, and that the outer drama was meant to show her what she was doing to herself.

Being compassionate means being truthful. How often do you rehearse in your mind what you are going to say to someone because you are justifying yourself, protecting your self-image, talking about how great you are or how right you are? Every time you find yourself mentally rehearsing a situation (as everyone does) ask, "Can I express one deeper level of truth?" You can always find at least one small way to be more loving, understanding, and compassionate.

Finding your deepest truth means looking within. It means not blaming other people, not playing the victim, and not spending time feeling sorry for yourself. When you look more deeply at any situation, you will discover that you set it up for your own growth. In any situation where you felt you were a victim, you always had an inkling of what was going on and ignored opportunities to change things.

As you look more deeply at things that really bother you, I propose a thought: Nothing you are upset about is caused by what you think it is. For instance, you may be upset that your friend accused you of doing something you did not do. Upon deeper examination, you will find that it is a re-creation of an earlier pain, played out over and over in changing scenery with different people until you resolve it. It may be a reenactment of a childhood drama in which someone accused you of things you did not do.

Strong reactions of pain, anger, or resentment you feel in present time are almost always caused by a childhood experience that evoked similar feelings. You re-create the pain so that you can evolve and move beyond it. Next time you feel angry at someone, stop. Close your eyes and go within. Acknowledge that you have had similar experiences or felt these emotions before. Realize that you are reliving some childhood decision or painful event, and that now is an opportunity to end this pattern in your life and instead experience your deepest truth. Realize that you draw other people into your life to play out certain roles with you that will help you evolve. Let go of any anger or blame you feel toward them.

You have the ability to know your truth.

The truth is that you are a great being; you have within you the compassion, courage, strength, and wisdom to live your life from a high level at all times. You act out roles that do not reflect the greatness of who you are, but they are only roles and not your true Self.

The more awareness you have of your thoughts, the more control you will have over the drama happening inside of you. You might think of your thoughts as little people who come marching up, one, two, three. If you could stop each one and hold it up to the light of your soul, you would find better ways of thinking. It is a matter of attention and awareness, examining each thought you have in order to become aware of whether or not it is really a true statement.

Speaking and acting from truth means paying attention to your energy. Often you do not notice what is happening until the situation is so painful you must go inward, meditate, think, and put yourself in another person's shoes. That may be the whole reason you created the situation. If you were to do these things frequently, life would be easier. If, when you felt uncomfortable, you went inward and opened your heart with compassion, things would not reach a crisis level.

Every time you rehearse in your mind what you will say to people, you are sending energy into your future interaction with them. Often you rehearse so that you can express a deeper and more compassionate level in your actual communication. If you can make this the goal of mental rehearsal, you will find your relationships clearing up.

If you are rehearsing to protect or justify yourself or get something from another person, you will find yourself uncomfortable when you are speaking to him or her. You will have an incomplete communication, one that may lead to further energy expenditure and perhaps further struggle. That is why, when you are angry with someone, it is better to wait until you can speak from the loving space of your deepest truth, rather than act out of anger.

Why is it so difficult to look another person in the eyes and express your deepest truth? Is it because you fear the other person will not love you if you reveal your deeper being? For some of you it is a fear of being vulnerable. It is often easier to play out roles that say, "I am strong and invincible, I am a perfect person," than to take down the walls and reveal who you are to another person. When you have nothing to lose, it certainly is easier to express your deepest truth.

The Universe may put you in a situation in which you have nothing to lose so that you can experience speaking your deepest truth, which can deepen your connection and lift the relationship to a new level. However, to speak the truth, you do not need to get to the point where you have nothing to lose.

Imagine in front of you, right now, anyone you would like to connect with to clear up an issue or make the relationship between you better. See the person's face in front of you, and his or her eyes looking at you with complete understanding and compassion. Picture the person accepting your truth. Mentally say something to him or her that will offer both of you an opportunity to feel more loving, connected, and at peace with each other.

As you think over
what you will say to someone,
hold the image of your deepest truth
and practice loving ways of expressing it.

Each time you rehearse, you become more efficient and confident, and you will find an even better way to express yourself. Be kind and gentle with yourself. When you first begin to speak truth, you may find there is a part of you that criticizes you for not having done it better.

If you find yourself reviewing past events, do not make yourself wrong for the way you spoke or acted. Instead, recognize that you did the best you knew how. You can send energy backward or forward, so that the energy you send from your heart can heal a situation in the past or make it better in the future. Recognize that what you learned opened up your truth.

At a certain level, everyone knows the truth about each other. You may not want to acknowledge that you are aware of the truth, but you do indeed know it at some level. There is no hiding from each other, and there is no need to do so. You are a magnificent, beautiful, alive human being doing the very best you can.

You evolve when you match your words and actions to your truth and awareness of who you are. You may think it is not kind to say what is on your mind, or to speak out if what you want to say requires asserting yourself or asking for what you need. You may think you are doing someone a favor by covering up your feelings, but you may be setting up a drama where the only way out is through acknowledging and living your truth. You may even have to end a relationship if that is what it takes to detach enough to speak the truth.

Honoring your deepest truth
is a great gift to you
and to the other person.

This does not mean that you should express truth by making the other person wrong. When you do speak your deepest truth, do so with love for yourself and for the other person. If what you say is damaging or harmful to the other person, then you have not come from your deepest truth, which is always loving.

For instance, a woman was dating a man who later left her for another woman. She was very hurt and, on the surface, wanted to strike out at him and make him feel bad about himself. Her first inclination, since she felt hurt and rejected, was to make him wrong. As she got in touch with her deeper truth, she realized that she truly loved him, wanted him to be a friend, and saw that what she had done in past relationships — close her heart and walk away — was not an expression of her truth. Even though she felt hurt, she was able to recognize the love underlying the pain and express that love in her communication. Within several months, the man came back to her, a new level of respect and love for her in his heart.

Many of you hold up an image of truth, and yet you deceive yourself about who you are. You do so when you imagine yourself as a victim, for you are not a victim; you are a high, powerful being. You deceive yourself anytime you do not acknowledge your beauty, wisdom, and power.

Anytime you find yourself sinking into feelings of self-pity or negativity, you are not living your deepest truth. When you deceive yourself by thinking of yourself as a victim, you carry that energy within you, and you will experience it played out in the world around you. If you are telling yourself that you are not powerful, you begin to set up a resonance in your energy field, and you attract people and events to you that mirror that thought. As you become truthful about who you are, so will the Universe reflect that truth.

Take a situation you want to improve with someone and imagine that the very wisest part of you — your highest being, your higher self, the confident, powerful, loving part of you —

is handling it. See a smile on the other person's face, and talk to the person in your mind.

Anytime you find yourself speaking in a way that is not confident and high, first acknowledge that you are doing the best you know how. Appreciate all the parts of yourself. It is not going to help you evolve if you make the high part right and the emotional part wrong. Keep focusing on the higher part of yourself and give love to the insecure part, and it will evolve.

Watch as you rehearse scenes in your mind. Observe yourself playing out your roles; look at the reaction you anticipate from the other person. Realize that you often get what you expect. Hold in your mind a vision of yourself speaking your truth in a most loving and compassionate way, putting yourself in the other person's shoes. Doing this is one of the highest and most loving things you can do for the relationship.

Imagine the other person responding with warm understanding. Also imagine that no matter how the other person responds, you will stay centered and balanced, in touch with your truth. A sense of joy and energy will surely follow, for it takes far more energy to withhold the truth, to deny and avoid it, than to recognize it and speak and act upon it.

Initially it may take energy to open up, but consider the overall results: the amount of time spent thinking about the situation and the pain you feel will be over. You will have hours of free time. What will you do with all that extra time?

You release creative energy when you free yourself from any situation that does not honor you and the truth of your being. As you speak, practice accuracy and precision with your words. Watch with care every statement you make and attitude you assume, in order to negate any tendency toward emotional misrepresentation. Do not overemphasize details or exaggerate the usual and commonplace into the unusual and uncommon. Develop the ability to produce a picture of things as they really are, and it will help you create what you want in physical reality.

As you match your words with the truth, your energy will go higher and higher. You will have more physical energy, more peace, and better connections with people. You will replace those friends who do not want to relate to you from a deeper truth with new friends who do. The old, uncomfortable situations you have set up will not be able to survive in your new level of light, and they will dissolve.

PLAYSHEET

Chapter 8

Finding Your Deepest Truth

1. Is there anyone in your life you have withheld truth from? Think about or jot down what you really want to say to him or her. Let it come out without judgment.
2. Now that you have thought about this or written it down, is there an even deeper level of truth you can access, one that is softer, more compassionate, and that acknowledges the other person as a loving individual? Think again about what you would like to say.
3. You can keep doing this until you discover the real issue between the two of you. Then imagine light and joy between you as you release the truth with love and compassion.

Journey into Light: Going Higher

There are many levels of energy in the Universe, from the coarser or denser levels all the way up to the levels of great mastery. The coarser levels exist as heavy emotions and negative thoughts. The higher levels are beyond polarities, beyond good and bad, beyond the storms of the emotions. They are levels of increasing love, light, and personal power. There are lessons at every level, and one of the easiest ways to go higher is to acknowledge the lessons as challenges and opportunities for growth.

As you go higher the challenges do not stop, but they do change in their nature. You could not grow without challenges, which are really opportunities. Your attitude toward them either helps you go higher and grow faster, or keeps you in the dense levels longer.

The more you dislike problems and the more you rebel against things not going your way, the longer your problems will stay with you. These denser levels of energy are like quicksand pulling you down. When you are caught in them, your thoughts revolve around what you consider to be problems.

As you move to higher levels, your thoughts move also, and you begin thinking about what your soul can accomplish, how your soul can evolve your personality, and how you can follow your spiritual path. Each of you in your own way seeks to know yourself.

To sense energy, you must know yourself, put energy and time into yourself, and become aware of who you are and what you are thinking. You can increase self-awareness by paying attention to your thoughts. Record them and divide them into categories. In each category, such as thoughts about a relationship, your career, abundance and money, daily activities, or spiritual growth, investigate how high your level of thinking is. Thoughts that are negative or self-destructive are on the dense, or lower, side; thoughts that are positive, optimistic, or loving are on the finer, higher side.

One way to move from denser energy levels into higher energy is through your will and intent. You can go higher by simply affirming that you intend to go higher. Battling with problems or struggling with issues can bog you down. Sometimes the mind loves to get involved in arguing, in resisting and struggling, which keeps you in the lower energies.

Every time you come to an issue that you cannot resolve, affirm to yourself that you have the will and intent to go higher. Ask your soul for assistance, to shine its light on the situation. Use your imagination to take you higher by creating a vision of what you want.

The ability to make yourself
right rather than wrong
will help you grow faster.

Learn to affirm that everything you do, whether you understand why or not, is perfect for your growth. Many of you have chosen a fast course of evolution, resolving to grow quickly all at once. You want to complete many parts of your soul's journey during this life, choosing a steep path of growth rather than a slow and gradual one.

Transformation of the planet begins in transformation of the self. Evolution starts with the commitment and intent to go higher. Pay attention to your thoughts and your emotions, and become aware of the messages in the challenges you are going through.

Avoid getting stuck in issues; look at them as if they were to your side rather than in front of you. Focus on what you want rather than what you do not want. Once you have demonstrated to the Universe that you intend to go higher, you will be flooded with new insights into what to do. The Universe will begin to show you the way.

Many of you feel that your struggles are insurmountable. You might have struggled to establish a deep love or the right connection with others. Some of you wrestle with your appearance, diet, nutrition, or exercise. Others of you feel trapped by having too many bills or a perceived lack of abundance.

You may debate with yourself, asking, "Is this the right way, or is that the right way?" All of you have the inner knowledge and wisdom to know what the right way is for you, if you listen to your inner self. You have an abundance of information available to you right now.

Perhaps one of the greatest challenges facing all of you is knowing what information to use and what information not to use. Information is flooding the planet. There are books to read, advice on what to eat, what not to eat, how to feel, how not to feel, how to grow spiritually, what to do, and what not to do. There is a great deal of confusion about all these facts. You may feel that if you could force yourself to eat all the right foods, follow all the rules, and work on yourself constantly, you would be a perfect, evolved person. The ego and the mind would prefer evolution to be structured and formulated; not so the soul.

Childhood programming and a desire to be part of the group teach you that what everyone else is doing is the right way. However, each of you is completely different. Your nutritional needs, exercise and sunlight requirements, relationships, desires, and financial and work needs are different.

*There is no one right way
to evolve or pursue your soul's path.
It is up to you to follow your inner guidance
about what is best for you.*

Awareness of your own energy will tell you what is good for you. When you look around at all the books you have in your home, hear about all those weight-loss processes, for instance, do not ask yourself, "What should I try?" Ask instead, "What would I love to do?" The things that you would love to do, books that you would delight in reading, and things you cannot wait to try are good for you. Those that you feel you should or must do are not appropriate for who you are.

You can use your willpower, as you call it, to make yourself, force yourself to, follow other people's programs, but always your inner being will undo it. Then you may label yourself a failure or feel you have no willpower. It is not willpower as you know it that will evolve you; it is the intent to go higher, and letting the changes come naturally, that will evolve you.

Allow your feelings to flow from moment to moment, act upon them, and know them. For instance, with food, simply become quiet and relaxed, and ask yourself what you crave and what sounds delicious. Even if you desire chocolate or something else you have labeled as bad for you, it may be that your physical body needs some substance in chocolate to maintain its sense of well-being and health, and the only way it knows how to acquire it is through chocolate. You may need only a little, and once you take away all the shoulds and should nots, you will find your body naturally craving other things that it needs.

When you speak of books — all the books you should read and the knowledge you should have — be aware that sometimes it is only one paragraph or one page of a book that you need to read to get the guidance or answer you seek. I am speaking of the quality of discernment, knowing the difference between what is good for you and what is not.

Each of you has a personal map of reality, your own assumptions, a unique philosophy about life, and a personal belief system. One of the challenges I offer you is to look at your map. What is a personal map? For one person a map may say, "There is not enough love in the world." For another, his or her map may say, "Every time I open up to another person, I get hurt." You base your maps on your childhood and lifetime experiences. You base them on your experience of how your energy has flowed out and how you have been received by others, especially those you loved or those you wanted love from.

If any area of your life
is not working,
one of your beliefs in that area
needs to be changed.

It is time to either get a new map or revise the one you have. You cannot change it by forcing yourself, however. You can change it by calmly and firmly telling yourself that you intend to go higher and that you do not plan to get caught up in the argument or the issues. It may sound too simple, but this is all you need to do to start moving out of conflict. Once you affirm that you intend to go higher, the Universe will begin to show you the answers.

Another way to move out of denser, negative energy is to be aware of the telepathic messages and emotions you send out, for they can affect many people. Whatever you send out is what you draw back in. Take responsibility for the thoughts and emotions you send out, for they go out into the world and create events and circumstances that come back to you.

You can learn how to send positive thoughts and emotions to other people or project them out into your own future where you can meet up with them. Every thought you send out is magnetic because it creates and brings to you events, people, and things. It attracts what you think about and determines what you draw to yourself.

You can assist humanity
in achieving peace
by evolving your thoughts.

Every thought you send out creates events in your world and attracts people to you. Even more than that, every thought you send out is creating the transformation of the planet. You may not feel that one person can have that much effect on the overall energy of the planet, and yet one high, healing thought filled with loving and peaceful energy can cancel out 10,000 or more negative ones. The higher the thought, the more potent it is, canceling out many lower ones.

It is not just yourself you are helping when you evolve your thoughts, but everyone around you as well. You do not even have to know people personally or be physically around them for your thoughts to affect them. Healing, positive thoughts go out into your neighborhood and your community and help everyone who is reaching upward and who is in resonance with your energy.

Imagine you are sitting up above the earth, as you have seen it from the satellite photos, and sense that a great deal of humanity below you is thinking about mundane things or is lost in lower thoughts. Know that the higher you go, the more people you can reach with your finer and higher thoughts. People going about their daily lives, looking for answers to their problems, can use the healing, loving broadcast you are sending out.

Humanity is going through a transformation. Humanity is at a crossroads — in one direction lies peace and abundance; in the other, conflict and scarcity. It is time to become aware of your personal thoughts on an ongoing, daily basis. Every time you hate something, every time you feel angry at yourself, every time you put yourself down or make yourself wrong, you are contributing to the planetary choice of scarcity. Every time you allow yourself to have more, permit yourself to feel good or love something, you are contributing to the planetary path of peace, love, and abundance.

PLAYSHEET

Chapter 9

Journey into Light: Going Higher

1. Make a physical or mental list of the main things you think about (career, friends, family, money, car, clothes, food, health, and so on). Rate how positive you feel about each of these things on a scale of 1 to 10 — 1 being negative, 10 being positive.
2. As you review or think about your list, how high and loving are your thoughts?
3. Take one area that you have negative or lower thoughts about and write down a positive picture of it that you could hold.

Learning Unconditional Love

Unconditional love means keeping your heart open all the time. To do so, you may need to let go of the expectations you have of other people, of wanting them to be anything other than what they are. It means letting go of any need for people to give you things, act in certain ways, or respond with love. Many of you wait for other people to be warm and loving before you are.

> *Unconditional love is learning*
> *to be the source of love*
> *rather than waiting for others*
> *to be the source.*

Unconditional love allows you to join with others and keep your personal boundaries intact. To be able to join with others, you need to know your own boundaries. People desire to join with others, to have loving connections, and yet at the same time to be separate.

If you are feeling suffocated in a relationship, if others are asking you to do things you do not want to do, it is because you are not clear about your own boundaries. Although it is easier to blame the other person, it is you who needs to get clear about your boundaries. On the other hand, if there are things you want from another person that you are not getting, it may be because you are trying to use the other person to fill a space within you that only you can fill.

Take the example of a woman who feels suffocated in a relationship. She feels the man she is with is constantly asking for more than she wants to give — more time, attention, and commitment to the relationship. She blames him for being so demanding. However, the pattern lies within her, and until she recognizes it, she will continue to attract similar relationships. Often a pattern shows up as its opposite. She may attract either men who demand too much or men who are unavailable and do not want an involvement.

This is a woman who has not come to terms with her sense of self. So long as she is not certain where she ends and other people begin, she will constantly be struggling to define her boundaries. She will shy away from commitments, because she experiences them as a loss of self-identity. Not having clarity about who she is, she will feel pressured by demands or even simple requests. If she had well-defined boundaries, she would find it easy to say no. If she had firm boundaries, she would not attract relationships that keep testing them. Once she has clarity about how much of herself she wants to give, and about what balance between herself and others feels right, she will attract relationships that fit this new picture.

Unconditional love transforms fear.

Fear is like a background noise that circles the planet, affecting many actions and decisions. It takes strength and courage to face what you fear. As you become aware of energy, you will also become aware of fear. The first place to examine it is in yourself, although it may be far more visible to you in other people. If, when you look at a friend or loved one, you can recognize where he or she is closed or fearful, notice whether it is a reflection of a place within you that needs more love.

It is easier to observe things in other people than in yourself. That is why the Universe will often teach you something about yourself by putting you around people who show you what you are learning. You would not focus on some particular trait or behavior if you were not working on that issue yourself.

Fear can come from your thinking patterns. There are common thoughts that tell you that you are bad or that if you do not watch out, you may be harmed. These are called universal beliefs because they are shared by many. You will at some point face them directly in yourself as you begin going upward into the higher levels of the Universe. Fear shows up in thoughts that are very self-critical — wondering if you have disappointed someone, thinking that you are not trying hard enough or that you yourself are not enough.

If you discover fears as you open to a new relationship, do not make yourself wrong. Fear is an undercurrent, and the more you can discover it and face it, the more you can heal it through your unconditional love and acceptance of yourself.

How do you discover fear? Look at some area of your life where you have a decision to make. Ask yourself if there are any reasons you do not feel free to make the decision to do what you want to do. Perhaps you fear that there will not be enough money, that you cannot make it on your own, that you will not succeed, or that others will not love you or want you if you do not live up to their expectations or if you stand up for yourself.

As you look at this decision, ask yourself what you would do if you knew you were totally protected, guided, and loved by the higher forces of the Universe. If you knew your soul was assisting you in every way possible, and if you knew you could fully trust your wiser self, would you make a different decision? This is one way of uncovering fear.

*Fear is a place that
has not yet discovered love.*

People often disguise fear as logical and rational reasons why they cannot do something. Sometimes fear comes disguised as a conviction that other people are stopping you from doing something you want to do. There are many ways to disguise fear — blame it on others, refuse to take responsibility, decide you cannot do it anyway so why try, or get angry and quit, among others. What ways do you use to cover up fear?

If you discover you are covering up fear in these or other ways, the first step is to recognize that the reason you are avoiding something or feeling bad about another and your-self is because of fear, and that it is a place that requires your unconditional love. Love this part of you; do not make it wrong.

Be willing to look directly at what you are avoiding. You do not have to apologize, cover up by acting strong, or think that you are a bad person. Once you recognize fear, it becomes much easier to deal with. It is only when it is in disguise that fear can create pain and struggle.

One way to discover fear is to think of something you want to create but fear you cannot, and list all the reasons why you cannot create it. Then, turn those reasons into positive statements of why you *can* create what you want. You will find that fear dissolves in the light of consciousness. Love is like the warm sun that shines on the ice: it melts any barriers, any areas of pain. Like the ice, your fears will turn to water and evaporate.

When you notice yourself responding to other people with fear rather than love, perhaps pulling away from them, afraid that they will reject you, make you wrong, or ask too much of you, thank yourself for becoming aware of fear. Love that part of you that is afraid, and then begin to radiate unconditional love.

When you are judgmental or critical, you are more affected by other people's energy. If you look at people and think, "They ought to work harder to get their lives in order," these thoughts pull their negative energy into you. What you pay attention to in other people is what increases in your experience of them, for as you focus on something, you draw it out. What you fear you draw to you. Get in touch with that gentle loving part of you, your higher and wiser self who guides you to be more loving.

When you experience uncomfortable barriers and boundaries between yourself and others, it is a sign that you need to transmit more love to others and to yourself. You may not choose to live with them, be close to them, or be around them all the time, but they will still benefit from your broadcast of love. Some of you try to put on a brave and strong front, acting in a way that says, "I will not be vulnerable or hurt."

Yet, that very act creates fear and pain, attracting even more negative actions from people, which then requires an even braver exterior.

Look at the times you want to close your heart, the times at which you say, "I have had enough; this person is not acting loving enough for me; I think I am going to leave." In every relationship, no matter how long-term or solid, it will always be a challenge to keep your heart open. How else do you learn unconditional love but by coming up against all those areas of your life in which your heart is closed?

Each time you experience a situation that makes you want to close your heart, you now have the opportunity to establish a new pattern and keep your heart open. You may still choose to leave or change the nature of the relationship, but you can do so with love. You may think that the best friends are those who never challenge you, who never make you want to close your heart. Yet, most relationships challenge you to remain open and loving, so that you can learn how to love even more completely and deeply. The heart always deals with issues of trusting, opening and reaching new levels of acceptance and understanding of others.

You learn to love by putting yourself
in situations that challenge you to be loving.

Tolerance is an attribute of unconditional love. Smiling inwardly when people do things that used to upset you, sending them a warm blessing or thought of love, frees you from being affected by their behavior. The quality of tolerance is the ability to stay calm and unruffled no matter what happens, to allow people to be themselves and make their own mistakes. It allows you to provide that warm, safe harbor for them where they can bask in the steadfast light of your acceptance.

Whatever you give others is also a gift to yourself.

The ability to accept other people for who they are is a great challenge, and as you master it, so do you give that gift to yourself. If someone is yelling at you or talking in a way or a tone of voice that sparks anger, defensiveness, or sadness in you, begin radiating love to him or her. Bring yourself to a peaceful center and relax your breathing. As you radiate love, do not expect the other person to quit yelling or respond to your love in any way. Know as you send this love you are raising your vibration. Soon, either the other person will change or you will find that you are no longer creating situations where others are angry at you.

Relationships challenge you to keep your heart open and feel loving toward others. The quality of defenselessness is important. It is that feeling that you have nothing to defend, hide, or apologize for. It comes from a feeling of self-acceptance — not from justifying behavior that you want to improve, but from knowing that making yourself wrong for it will only lock you into that behavior longer.

People are often afraid to admit that they may be wrong, are struggling with things, or are in pain. Sometimes, for instance, when you are feeling unsettled and out of your calm, clear center, you may try to put on a front, acting as if nothing is wrong. If instead, when you are with another, you allow yourself to express your true feelings, you open up a channel of communication that can deepen your connection.

You may want everybody to think you are a perfect person, so you act out a role that says, "I am fine; do not worry about me. I am tough and I do not need any help." That creates separateness between yourself and others and keeps you from love at the very time you most need it.

Have you noticed how much love you feel toward others when they are vulnerable and admit that they are not sure how to handle something, rather than acting as if they know it all? Do not be afraid to let others recognize you for who you are.

If you have nothing to defend,
life becomes easier, for you do not
have to pretend to be anything you are not.

Life is harder when you think you have to defend your beliefs, thoughts, or self. Most of the things you think you have to defend are beliefs and ideas that are not yours anyway. You rarely get offended and hurt when someone disagrees with the things you are sure about. The areas where you are not certain, where you feel insecure, are those you often feel the most need to defend.

The next time you feel you have to defend something about yourself, ask yourself, "Why am I feeling I must defend this?" Be willing to let your heart and wisdom smile upon people, sending them your love and acceptance. Do not feel you must say anything. Be who you are. If you do not know the answer to something, simply say, "I do not know." Do not try to be perfect all the time. Do not think that to be loved you must have all the answers, that you must never be afraid or look weak, for if you are willing to be vulnerable you will find more love coming to you.

Forgiveness is a part of unconditional love. Forgive yourself throughout the day for all the moments when you are not high, loving, or wise. Forgive others for all the moments they are not high, loving, or wise. As you forgive, you make it easier to become those things you want to be, and you make it easier for others to become what they want to be as well.

People who respond to you in a way that seems to deny that you are a loving being are usually experiencing fear within themselves. If they ignore you, make you wrong, say unkind things, or act in a way that implies you are not their equal, realize that they are acting out of fear. You do not need to respond to the fear within them by creating it within yourself. Instead, you can become a source of love and healing to those around you.

You attract situations into your life to learn from them. One way to change every situation for the better is by responding with love. As you do so, the nature and character of every situation will change. By practicing, you can learn to stay in a state of love for longer and longer periods of time. Practice everywhere you go. Send love to the earth. Send love to everyone you meet. See if you can notice something beautiful about them.

Love brings beauty
to everything and everyone.
Most of all, love brings beauty to you.

When people are in pain, it is a powerful time to offer them support to change their lives. Often when they are afraid, they are also ready to listen. If you perceive that people are afraid, that they do not feel loving toward themselves, it may be time to reach out, send them your unconditional acceptance, and embrace them in your light.

Those who appear to have no fear, who seem to be the bravest, may need even more love than people who are willing to be vulnerable. Those who create pain in others, who are aggressive, bully other people, and make life miserable for those around them, are usually the most in need of love. Send love to those who seem to have everything and to those who seem to have power over you, such as your landlord, boss, or parents. They have power over you only to the degree to which you let them; only your fear can create a sense of inferiority in you.

If in any way you fear people in a position of authority or power over you, send them love. It will help stop any power struggles and attune you to a higher part of their being, where miracles and love are available.

As you become filled with light,
your power to affect the
world around you increases.

If people in your life are sending out negative energy and not meeting your expectations, it is important to send them unconditional love. They are simply being themselves, doing the best they know how. You will find great inner peace when you do not need others to act in a certain way in order to be happy yourself. You will become a radiating beacon of energy.

The higher you go, the more people you can affect with your love and good thoughts. When you send someone uncon-ditional love, it is no longer possible for you to be affected by his or her negative energy. If there is any situation in your life where you are feeling hurt, afraid, or separated from others, begin sending them love and acceptance for who they are. This will help you and them.

The more people act mean, the more they are afraid and the more they need your love. Indeed those who are humble, vulnerable, and defenseless most often have at their disposal an abundance of love. Offer love to them, too, but do not forget to send your love to those who appear to be the most unlovable, for they are the ones who are crying out the loudest for love.

Find reasons to love the unlovable, to care for people who act in destructive ways. There is not one person alive who does not grow from being loved. Whenever you give love, it comes right back to you, and you become magnetic to even more love. It may not come from those you are sending love to, but it will come.

When you are feeling afraid for any reason, it is a time to connect with your higher self. When you felt afraid as a child, there was usually someone or something that reassured you and took away the fear — a loving parent, a caring relative, or a favorite stuffed animal. It was often something outside of you, however.

Part of your journey into light is to learn to create inside yourself that sense of safety, that assurance that the world is friendly and that you are loved and protected by a caring and supportive Universe. Ask your higher self to assist you. Calm your breathing and go inward until you find that place of trust.

When you are afraid, imagine that you are being embraced by the most loving friend you have ever had, one who cares for you unconditionally, who loves you whether you have high thoughts or low, who is by your side all the time, and who offers you constant light. This is your higher self, your soul.

Know that you have this friend you can call upon when you are afraid, one who will help you experience the confident, secure, and courageous parts of yourself. You can also call upon the guides and masters, for your call is always heard, and love and guidance are immediately sent in response. All you need do is ask for help and it will be there.

Even when things seem uncomfortable and appear to not be going your way, do not think you are off your path, for you are always reaching upward. Sometimes it may seem difficult and the path may feel steep. Other times you may find yourself symbolically running, dancing, and traveling through your life with ease. Suspend judgment and make each stage of your growth easier by accepting what comes.

Allow yourself to love the bumpy road as well as the smooth one. Constantly thank yourself for your courage in reaching upward, in trying to express the highest and best of yourself that you can. Remember that you are a loving being, that you deserve love, and that you are, in essence, love itself.

PLAYSHEET

Chapter 10

Learning Unconditional Love

1. Think of an area in your life you would like to change. Record or note what changes you would make. (For example, "I would like to spend more time in nature," and so on.)

2. List all the reasons you cannot possibly create that change. These represent your unconscious fears. (For example, "I cannot possibly spend time in nature; I have too much to do that requires me to be indoors.")

3. Sit quietly and forgive every part of you that does not think you can create this change. Send love and acceptance to all these doubtful, fearful voices.

4. Turn these doubts into positive affirmations and begin saying them to yourself. You might want to write them down and put them where you can view them every day for a few weeks. (For instance, "I can now spend all the time I want in nature.")

Handling Pain by Choosing to Grow

A s you move to the higher levels of awareness, you may be faced with handling the energy of anger and pain within others and in yourself. Learning how to stay balanced and in your heart while in the presence of those energies is part of the soul's evolution toward light.

When you feel hurt and separated from another person, thinking he or she caused you pain or unhappiness, it may be time to examine what lessons you have chosen to learn by creating the situation. When you love people, there are times you feel pain and distance from them. If this happens, do not look for intellectual reasons.

Do not try to discover who has hurt the other, and who is to blame and who is in the right. It rarely does any good to argue back and forth, figuring out who is the good person and who is the bad person. This puts you into a power struggle with each other and takes you out of your heart connection.

Both people usually feel they are right and that the other person is unjustified in his or her approach. People usually feel that their own anger is justified and that the other person's is not. When people feel hurt, most lash out at the other person as the cause of their pain. However, there is always pain inside before another can trigger it; the other person only acts as a catalyst. The other person is not the cause. The cause is pain within you. It is not an accident that the other person triggered it, either, for most often you choose to be around loved ones and friends who know how to upset you so that you may learn and grow.

When you find yourself feeling hurt and righteously indignant, sure that you are the injured party and that someone owes you an apology, be silent for a moment before you lash out in anger. It is very easy to feel righteous, and yet righteousness separates you from those you want to love and feel close to.

As you reach for more light, one of your lessons may be to learn not to make things right or wrong but to stay in your heart and offer compassion to yourself and to the other person. This involves being willing to acknowledge the other person's right to a different viewpoint and not feel you have to prove anything.

It is important to learn how to handle pain, for in doing so you allow your soul to become the captain of the ship. What is pain? Pain is an area in which you are not yet able to experience your soul's love. Pain is an area waiting for love.

Besides a natural tendency to blame another, there may be a tendency to retreat when you are in pain, to withdraw and close your heart. If you feel you are not being treated in a way you would like by a friend or a loved one, and that is causing you pain, it is better not to start by making him or her wrong and seeking an apology. Instead, start by looking within.

Another person can trigger pain only when there is already pain within you. He or she can cause you to close your heart only where your heart already wants to remain closed. If there is no pain within, another cannot bring it out. You would only feel compassionate and sorry for him or her, not angry and threatened.

> *Pain can be triggered by*
> *another person only when there is*
> *already pain within you.*

It is a gift every time another person creates pain in you. It is showing you an area in which your heart has not yet learned to be open. It is showing you a place where you may bring more light into yourself. You have drawn certain people into your life to show you the places where you need to become more open. Part of your lesson is to stay open and loving even when others are acting in a way that used to cause you pain.

Before you approach the other person with recrimination, closing your heart and pulling away, creating more separateness and pain, stop. Ask yourself if you are willing to bring in light.

How does one bring in light when there is pain? First of all, if you are in the middle of an argument, it is important that you get away from the physical presence of the person causing you pain while you begin to strengthen and draw light into yourself. Being physically near the other person (until you are quite a master at controlling energy) puts you in his or her aura. If the other person is in pain or is creating pain for you, being around him or her will make it harder to restore your own balance.

If you find yourself in the midst of an argument, if you find yourself feeling hurt, wanting to strike out or withdraw, first put physical distance between you. Keep your silence until you have had an opportunity to be alone. Ask for a few moments to sit and think. Say that you do not want to speak in anger. Often it helps diffuse the situation to explain that you would like to be more aware and compassionate and that you need a few moments away to compose yourself.

When you strike out at another, it is often because you are not feeling good inside about yourself. Recognize that when others create pain within you, when they seem to strike out at you, it is because they do not feel good inside about themselves, either.

Learn to stop talking when the energy grows heavy and dense between you and another. If you can create physical distance, do so. You can then bring in light by sitting quietly, imagining peace. It may be difficult to imagine peace when you are feeling angry. Try imagining beautiful scenery, a good memory, or something that will restore a sense of balance. Then, invite your soul into your heart. Ask it to awaken the highest consciousness possible of yourself as a loving being.

You may begin to feel an intensification of peace, and you may begin to feel sorry for what you have done or said. You may experience a sense that the whole issue got blown out of proportion, or that you did not mean the things you said. Or you may at this point be able to view the other person's anger or pain with compassion and detachment, not feeling personally responsible for his or her reaction. You may realize the other person got carried away and said things he or she did not mean.

*The more you understand
what you are learning from a situation,
the more rapidly you can leave it.*

Ask yourself what lessons you are learning from being with this person, or what growth you are accomplishing by being in this situation. Pain always signifies major opportunities for growth. Suppose, for instance, you are in pain because someone does not return your love to the degree you would like. It may be that you are learning to keep your heart open no matter what the other person does. It may be that you are learning about humility, harmlessness, and lack of self-importance.

Grow quiet and ask your soul to show you the lessons you are learning. Your soul will always respond. Over time you may realize that what has happened is a great gift even though at the time it may seem like a disappointment or even a tragedy. Ask your soul to show you the gift that this or any situation is offering you. The degree to which you feel pain is often an indication of the size of the gift that awaits you when you understand why you set it up.

Understanding is not enough by itself, however. Once you begin to understand what you are to learn, it is important to act upon it. Some of you feel pain and feel separate from others when they do not return your love, or when you have pictures and expectations that are not met. Try not to make those people wrong; doing so can escalate a power struggle between you. You cannot find answers when you are in a power struggle. Instead, as you grow silent and calm your energy, imagine that you are embracing these people with love, forgiving them no matter what.

Pain is a powerful indicator of growth, and it can be changed with love.

When you are in pain, you may find that the doorway to your soul is more available to you than at other times. During those times, you turn to your soul and ask for assistance. When you are open and seeking help from your soul, you can receive more of the love and guidance your soul is always offering you. As you learn to become more aware of energy and to experience it more directly, the challenge will be to stay in your heart and focus upon what is higher and finer in others rather than what is lower.

When you feel pain, it is an indication that some area of your life is not working; some belief, thought, or emotion is crying out to be loved and healed by your soul. Do not make yourself wrong or think of yourself as a bad person, but recognize it as an opportunity to examine, experience, and heal that area of your life by opening to your soul's love.

When people are angry with you, it is often an expression of their pain. Most people believe that they get angry only with just cause, and get hurt only when someone lets them down, aggravates them, rejects them, or makes unreasonable demands. However, people also use anger to control others. Is your fear of people's anger controlling your behavior around them? Do you use a threat of anger to control others?

When people get angry with you, or appear to want to hurt you, they may be doing it because they are in pain themselves. Because of their programs and upbringing, because of the way they look at the world, some people may think you have hurt them when you had no intention to do so. Sometimes people get angry when all you are doing is expressing an opinion that differs from theirs or stating a preference of your own. Be sure you are not acting on a desire to control or manipulate. Do not let their anger trigger pain within you.

Often two people hurt each other when each only wanted the other's love. Sometimes when people are hurt, what they really want is for you to offer them gentleness, love, and understanding. How difficult it is to be gentle and loving when someone is acting in a way that triggers pain within you!

It is part of learning to work with energy, however, to stop, soften your heart, and listen when you are around hurt or angry energy. It is tempting to grow defensive, to get angry yourself, or to lash out at the people who are hurting you. You may feel that they are trying to make you wrong, diminish you, or put you down. Often separation comes from feeling defensive, feeling that you must protect your pride or dignity at all costs.

When you are in pain or your feelings are hurt, what you really want from others is for them to listen to you, be gentle with you, and understand that you are upset. You do not want them to withdraw and get defensive. You do not want them to get upset with you when you are angry, but instead to recognize that you are hurt. Some of you yell at other people when you feel that they have hurt you. What you really want them to do is say with conviction, "Yes, I see. I am sorry I hurt you."

*If others express anger with you
or withhold their love in some way,
do not let their negativity
become a part of your response.*

When people are causing you pain or are getting angry with you, realize that what they want from you is for you to love them. They do not want you to withdraw, get angry, feel hurt, or defend yourself. In truth, the issue rarely even matters to them. They are experiencing their own pain and it has nothing to do with you. Although they may blame it on you or tell you it is your fault, any pain they blame on you comes from pain within them, from places within their hearts that are not yet open.

As you become more telepathic, you will be able to sense the pain in others even more, and that is why you will want to stay in your heart. As you view humanity from the higher realms, you will become aware that there is much pain, anger, and negativity. Yet, there is also much beauty, love, and goodwill.

As you begin to open to a greater awareness of the energy around you, you will also begin to open to an awareness of your own energy. You may observe things in yourself that you want to change. It is important not to make wrong the things you detect, for your soul will not continue to reveal them to you if you do. Instead, know that your soul reveals to you those areas so that you may begin to bring the light of consciousness and the love of your heart into them.

When people get angry at you, stand back. Realize that they do not know a better way to let go of their pain than to speak of it or to blame others for causing it. If they are saying that you did something wrong, that you are bad, that you hurt them or caused them grief, do not attach yourself to their words. Do not think that you are responsible. They are responsible for their own upset or anger. You may have acted as a catalyst, but the pain had to be within them first. So, as they express their anger, do not start arguing or defending yourself; simply remain silent, hold open your heart, and focus your love on them.

As they speak and get it all out, there may be a great temptation to jump in and tell them they are wrong, that you have not acted in such a manner as they are describing. Hold your tongue, for in the end, you will be grateful. Let them express their energy without putting anger out yourself. Once they have said it all, you will still be in a loving and balanced space, feeling good about yourself. You will have mastered one of the most difficult of lessons — staying balanced in the presence of anger and pain.

> *If you have trouble forgiving people,*
> *pretend that the next time*
> *you talk to them is*
> *their last day on earth.*

Perhaps a person has caused you pain. Imagine as you go to be with him or her that it is this person's last day on earth. See how much you really appreciate who this person is, the gifts and the love he or she has sent your way. See that it would be easy to let go of any pain and come from a high level if you knew this would be his or her last day. You would be able to come from your heart, no matter how the person acted. You would be generous, warm, and loving.

When you do see this person again, pretend this meeting will be your last. Notice how you become aware of wonderful things about him or her — the light and love that is there. Recognize that this person had no real intention to hurt you, that he or she was acting the way he or she did in response to his or her own pain, confusion, or lack of clarity. Perhaps you did something that particularly upset this person, and he or she was simply reacting, like a robot at times, to a program of pain within.

You can embrace this high perspective. You can make every connection high and loving. Picture in your mind how you would act toward various people in your life if you knew you had only one more chance to be together. Since you are not going to be with them again, you can more easily send them telepathic messages saying that you absolutely forgive them, and then send them love.

Imagine that you have one day left to clear up any of the silent or spoken messages you have sent them. Even if they have pulled away and left you, if there are unresolved issues between you, you can still clear them up. If someone has died and left you, and there was anger between you, your decision to forgive will reach that person's soul. If there is someone who has passed on that you would like forgiveness from, ask for his or her forgiveness. This person may be trying to send you forgiveness, and all you need do is open to receive it.

If you are experiencing a painful situation with someone, release the pain within before you speak to him or her. Take all the time alone you need to get into a peaceful, higher state. When you do connect, sit quietly with them, not rehashing the situation, not going into the details, but instead simply sitting in peace together. Tell them that you know they did not mean to hurt you, that you understand their position. Be loving, and the pain will disappear.

Even when you have decided to operate from a higher level and be more loving, you may not be able to do it for very long the first time you are with a person after a fight or disagreement. Set a limit in your mind on the amount of time you think you can be around this person and still maintain a peaceful, loving stance.

If you have been in a difficult situation with someone, do not arrange to spend four or five hours with him or her in this first attempt to be your new higher and more loving self. Arrange for a brief contact, a length of time in which you know you can maintain a higher focus. If you are living with this person, find things to do that keep you busy and away from him or her until you are ready to connect.

If you have fought with or otherwise experienced negative energy with someone, or have had someone withdraw from you, the next time you connect with the person do so in a way, and at a time and in a place, that will support you in maintaining a more loving perspective. When you sense that you are closing down, falling into anger or pain, find an excuse to leave. You will discover through practice that this becomes easier, that you can hold a higher focus with people for longer periods of time, until you are naturally and automatically able to do so. You will gradually experience a new, more loving, and higher you.

PLAYSHEET

Chapter 11

Handling Pain by Choosing to Grow

1. If there is a situation in your life right now that is causing you pain or hurt, if you feel angry at another or someone is angry at you, write it down or make a mental note of it.
2. Sit quietly and invite in your soul. Fill your mind with peaceful thoughts. Imagine that you are rising to a higher, lighter, and more peaceful level. Ask your soul to show you what you have been learning from this situation. (See the other person as volunteering to act out this role in order to teach you something you need to learn or evolve within yourself.) Write down your thoughts or make a mental note of them.
3. Imagine that the next time you are with this person will be your last time together — possibly his or her last day on earth. Imagine also that you are the most secure, loving, compassionate, and wise person you know. What would you say to him or her that would heal the situation and create love between you?

Opening Your Intuition

What is intuition, and how does it operate? Sometimes it is easier to explain intuition by saying what it is not. It is not the mind that figures everything out. It does not work like a computer going a + b + c = d. It does not utilize the principles of logic, as a computer does. Intuition is not ego; it does not operate in a world of form and structure.

Intuition is the ability to know without words, to sense the truth without explanations. Intuition operates beyond time and space; it is a link to your higher self. Intuition is not bound by the physical body. It operates knowing that the past, present, and future are simultaneous, happening in the "now" moment. It is the voice of your innermost Self, your soul, which is always looking out for you. It speaks to you through insights, revelations, and urges. It does not say to you, as the intellect would, "I must do this tomorrow; this is on my list; this would be a good thing if I got it done." Instead, intuition says, "Wouldn't it be fun, wouldn't it be joyful? This is what I want to do today."

Often intuition feels like the playful child within you, trying to lure you away from your hard work to the world of joy and play with its strong inner urges. Amazingly, in that playful world you can connect with all the answers you spent months working to find.

Intuition can synthesize ideas in a flash. Geniuses like Edison and Einstein worked at a very refined and high level of intuition. They brought in their ideas from outside of time and space. Intuition goes beyond that which is known into the unknown. It can help you find answers and information that are not known in the mind of another person. The challenge is to hear your intuition and then to follow it with action.

Many doors will open
when you follow your intuition.

You can find answers in a second to problems you have been working on for years. Perhaps you want to leave a job and your intellect keeps telling you, "If you leave you will starve; there is not enough money; you cannot do it." Meanwhile your intuition is saying, "Well, why don't you pretend you can do it — maybe there is a miracle or two out there that will make it happen." To bridge the gap between intellect and intuition, use the heart energy of trust and faith. Intuition will often give you answers that do not seem logical, yet the answers work if you trust them and act upon them.

How can you develop your intuition? First, learn to trust it. All of you have ideas about what you would like to do and be. You do have a vision of a more fulfilling life for yourself, although some of you do not allow yourselves to fantasize about that vision very often, and even fewer of you trust it enough to bring it into your daily experience.

How do you tell the difference between your desire for a certain inner message, and true intuition, which is guiding you to a higher future, to making the best possible choices? True intuition comes from your soul, and its guidance and insights come with conviction. These carry with them the energy, motivation, enthusiasm, and everything else that you need to put your intuitive insights into action.

There are some traps in living too much in the world of intuition. One is that intuition can operate in future time. Future ideas can dazzle you so that the present, in contrast, seems mundane and boring. There is a difference between physical reality, mental reality, and the realm of the intuition. The physical world is composed of much slower energy than the world of your thoughts.

Your intuition comes from an even higher, finer realm: that of your soul. With intuition, and then your mind, you can receive an idea, think about it, plan it out, carry it all the way through to fruition, and live it in a flash. Carrying it through in physical reality is much more time-consuming, for the world of physical reality involves form and time.

It can be much more fun to receive and think about ideas and intuitive insights than to actually take action on them. If you want to translate your intuition into physical reality, develop the qualities of patience, trust, confidence, and focus.

All of you have the ability to use your intuition and follow your hunches. Sometimes you get inner guidance or a feeling that tells you to stop doing something and work on something else instead. That is intuition. Only when you act upon your intuitive guidance and insights will you gain the fruits of the gifts that your intuition offers — in this case taking action means stopping what you are doing and working on whatever else you feel guided to do.

You can create your goals by acting on your intuition.

If you live on the intellectual level, you may have lists of things you should do. (Listen to that word *should*.) You might have your day, week, and month planned. Then you wonder why you do not feel joyful and free!

You may be living too much in the world of the intellect. Intellect and intuition have also been called the left brain and right brain. The left brain is the part of you that memorizes, deals with logic, and thinks in a time-oriented, sequential manner. The right brain is intuition and feelings, creativity and imagination — the world beyond words.

It is not enough to live in the world of intuition, for people who live there will do nothing with their lives other than daydream and fantasize and perhaps talk big. You have seen people who talk on and on of their big visions and plans and yet live in poverty and have not created anything.

It takes much focus, patience, will, and intent to bring intuition into reality. In physical reality, the minute you conceive of an idea, it is already old. That is why it is important to honor those things you have worked on in the past, to love yourself in the past. Everything is instantly in the past the minute it comes through your intuition into consciousness, the minute you hear it. Honor who you were and where you have come from; honor and love your past.

Many of you have a tendency to put yourself down because of who you were in the past. If you are writing a book, for instance, you may not like what you wrote a year ago. If you are in a career that is moving upward, you may look back and say, "I was only a _____ two or three years ago."

The more you can honor your past self, the more quickly you will be able to hear the voice of your intuition and move into your future. It is difficult to hear your intuition if you do not love who you were, for intuition opens to the degree to which you can love those forms you developed in the past. The more you love what you created in the past, the more you can operate at a higher level of intuition.

Send loving energy to your past.

It is important to go back and clean up your memories, for often the ego will bring you unwanted negative memories of the past that will hold you back. Recognize the soul qualities you were developing during painful times, and affirm that you were doing the best you knew how to do. The insights, skills, and attitudes you have today were developed during those times.

Each lesson left you with the growth that made the next step possible. How often do you think of the wonderful things you have accomplished? You already have memories of successfully doing anything you want to accomplish; thinking of them will help you achieve success now. If you do not have the exact memory, you do have enough similar experiences, which, when put together, can help you.

If you want to make the visions of your intuition real, you must first capture its images, slow them down, hold them in your mind, and then be patient enough to put them into action. The moment you capture your intuition, its vision becomes a memory and in this way becomes the past. It is important to remember the past with positive thoughts, for it contains the visions you are bringing into reality now.

Think back to the "should do" lists made by your intellect. You can spend weeks and months, even years, trying to map out your future at the mental level, thinking every step through. It is valuable to have a plan in that it gives you the faith and belief that you can achieve your goals. The most important thing is to hold a steady vision of your goals. If you follow the plan too rigidly, though, you deny the miracles and the creative flow of energy within you.

It is always faster and easier to create what you want by following your intuition. It can bring you, in its playfulness, all the goals and visions of your intellect and, usually, even more. Intuition may say, "Let us not do anything today; let us take a walk; let us go to the woods; let us go to the bookstore; let us indulge in something very unproductive." Then, lo and behold, at the end of the day you have produced more toward your higher goals than you would have by doing everything on your list. Perhaps you found an idea that helped you reach your goals six months sooner than you expected — for intuition guides you to your highest future in the most effective and efficient way.

Many of you would prefer to live in the future rather than in the present or the past. Remember, it is one thing to live in the future and bring back those visions to the present time, and another to never act upon those visions. If you do not act upon your visions, you will not be able to create the life you want.

The best way to develop your intuition is to listen to it.

Have you been hearing whispers in your mind that you have been ignoring? For instance, you may have heard whispers of what you would like to do for a career, but constantly create reasons why you cannot do it. Would it not be simpler to create reasons why you can? It takes far more energy to hold yourself back than to allow yourself to move forward. Think how drained you feel when you dwell on the negative, and how energized you feel, and how easily things move, when you dwell on the positive.

You may really want to quit your job and pursue a hobby or longtime interest. You may find your mind whispering to you that it will work. You may hear of other people succeeding in your field, and find all kinds of indications from the Universe that this is the right way to go. Intuition beckons you to the future with things you feel drawn to because you love them. When you follow that voice, you will find doors opening everywhere. If you are finding closed doors, it is the Universe telling you there is a better way to go. Do not keep pushing against closed doors; look around for the open ones.

Intuition talks to you through urges, flashes of ideas, insights, and feelings; it moves you in certain directions. To hear it, pay attention to your inner world of ideas and feelings. If you are forcing yourself to do one thing while your feelings are urging you to do something else, you are not paying attention to your intuition. Your intuition sends you messages constantly, telling you every moment what to do to open your energy. It is always directing you toward aliveness and a higher path.

Your intellect may do battle with your intuition. You have been taught to honor your intellect, through your culture, through science, and through the academic world, which are usually oriented to developing the rational, logical mind. Yet, many of humanity's greatest inventions — radio, electric lights, television, computers, and phones — have come from a synthesis of intellect and intuition.

The intellect can be highly developed; it loves to run the show. It can also feel threatened by intuition. Many of you have beliefs that say, "If it happens too easily, it is not right." Or, "If I do not work hard at it, the results are not valuable."

*When you operate
from intuition, things
happen more easily.*

Your intellect loves to plan everything out in a logical way; your intuition is spontaneous. Being flexible is important. If you rigidly stick to your preplanned goals, you may miss many messages from your intuition telling you how to make things simpler.

If you find yourself resisting doing something, stop and ask yourself what you would rather do instead. It may be that it is not the highest way to go, or it may be the wrong time. If you trust and act upon your feelings from moment to moment, you will be flowing with your intuition and the Universe.

There is a role for the intellect, and that is to formulate plans, to decide where to go, and to take action. The intellect is like the captain of a ship, consulting maps, making plans, and steering the ship. Yet, the weather and the ocean actually determine the course; the captain must remain flexible and use his or her plans as a guideline.

So it is with the intellect that steers your ship. Intuition tells you of storms ahead, of detours (that turn out to be shortcuts); it monitors a future path designed to bring you your highest good. Use your intellect to set goals, to aim you higher. Focus your will and intent on going higher. Your intuition will show you how to get there in the best, fastest, and easiest way if you follow your feelings, hunches, inner urges, and deeper desires.

For example, take the person who wants a new career. If he or she were to let go and keep picturing it, intuition would guide him or her to it. One day, while following a playful urge to go walking, this person might run into another person and the connection would furnish him or her with an idea or opportunity that would provide a starting point. Intellect may try to build a path logically, and may not recognize other ways things could work. It takes a great deal of trust to follow your feelings and intuition, for intuition usually shows you only one step at a time.

You can open your intuition by learning to listen to your feelings and act upon them. When you have an urge to do something, do it. Do not force yourself to go to a job you do not like; listen to your feelings. Be open to new ways to earn a living. Acting upon your feelings may take a leap of faith. Look back at all the times you have listened to those inner urges, acted upon them, and were amazed at your success.

Acting upon intuition also requires flexibility and spontaneity. Remember times in which you were flexible and let go of your plans, and things worked out wonderfully.

If you want to increase productivity, allow yourself to listen to your whispers and to act upon them. Allow yourself to play. Do those things you have been wanting to do. Be a child again. Create fun in your life, and you will find that your creative energy will awaken and flow as never before.

PLAYSHEET

Chapter 12

Opening Your Intuition

1. Write down or reflect upon three times you followed your intuition in the past — perhaps when you acted on a feeling, hunch, or urge and things turned out well.
2. Write down or think about at least three things your mind has been whispering or maybe even shouting to you to do. These could be small or big things.
3. Ask your soul for intuitive guidance about one step you could take toward each of those things to bring it into your life. Let this guidance come into your mind now or in the future. Remember that you have asked for this guidance, and recognize it when it comes.
4. When you receive guidance on one of these issues, set a date — if it is appropriate to do so — for when you will take action to implement it.

Your Mind, Inner Dialogue, and Personal Broadcast

Your mind puts out a powerful broadcast of energy. It also determines how you experience the world and what you create. Your thoughts are magnetic; they go out from you and draw to you those things you think about. Your inner dialogue is important, for the way you speak to yourself determines the events, people, and objects you attract.

To create happier events in your life and to live a more fulfilling life, it is important to use higher words and thoughts when you speak to yourself or others. Your thoughts create reality; they go out into the world and affect other people. As you move into the higher realms of energy, you will want to raise your thoughts by increasing their quality. As you begin thinking purer, kinder, and more loving thoughts, you will begin to change the magnetism of your body and resonate with the higher realms of the Universe.

You can begin by watching your inner dialogue. Do you make yourself wrong frequently? Do you tell yourself that your efforts are not enough? Are you always trying to rush, to hurry up, to make self-imposed and unreasonable deadlines? Are you always trying to please other people, telling yourself that if anyone is unhappy it is your fault and you have failed? Are you critical, finding fault with things, looking for what is not working and not right, rather than seeing the good in people and the situation?

Learning to control your inner dialogue is learning to make your mind obey rather than control you. It is learning to choose what thoughts come into your mind, rather than allowing yourself to be ruled by thoughts that randomly pop up. It is choosing whether you pay attention to the unwanted thoughts running through your mind or keep your mind still and focused upward.

Part of the goal of evolution is to bring the mind into the dominion of the soul. By watching your inner dialogue, loving yourself, and forgiving yourself for all your mistakes (which you can best view as learning experiences), you raise the level of your thinking. Notice what words you use and how you feel as you say them.

*Saying high, loving words
over and over raises
your mind's vibration.*

If you cannot focus for a long period of time on a certain thought, do not worry. It can take years of ongoing observation, intent, and working with your soul to bring the mind to a point of stillness and focus. Each time you succeed in focusing on higher ideals and thoughts for even a moment, congratulate yourself. Ask your soul to assist you in remembering to turn your attention to higher thoughts. Look for words that make you feel good when you say them to yourself.

If you notice yourself feeling anxious or depressed, use positive words to raise your energy. You can say uplifting words to experience higher levels of your being such as love, clarity, will, wisdom, and peace. You can say to yourself words such as "I am strong, giving, caring, committed, abundant, radiant, light, enthusiastic, peaceful, tranquil, and serene."

Think of all the beautiful, inspiring words you know. When you say the word *peace*, you open to the vibration of peace that exists in millions of minds throughout the world.

You connect with peaceful thoughts and events, for the outer world has much peaceful energy you can tune in to. Use positive, high words when you speak to yourself, words such as *effortless*, *inspired*, and *creative*. Make conscious use of these higher words. If you are feeling bad, simply say them over and over and you will begin to change your thoughts.

When you speak to yourself, use words that indicate present tense. Instead of saying, "Someday I will," say, "I am now." The mind interprets what you say to yourself literally. If you say, "I will be happy," your mind takes that literally and creates what you want, not as an event you experience now, but as something that will happen in the future. (Which means you will never experience it.) Watch that you do not put *anything* you want now into future tense; instead, speak of it as something you already have: "I love myself as I am today. I am happy today. I have money now. I have my soul mate now." It may not appear to be true as you say it, but it will be shortly.

If you say, "I am not enough," your mind takes that statement and begins to create outer events in which you experience yourself as not enough. Imagine that 40,000 to 50,000 thoughts go through your mind every day. If you can turn even 2,000 of them into thoughts of light, love, abundance, and joy, you will rapidly change what you experience. Within a month your experience of your life will be very different. It does not take that many high and loving thoughts to change your experience, for high and loving thoughts are many times more powerful than thoughts of a lower nature.

> *Talk of the qualities*
> *you aspire to as if*
> *you already have them.*

If you aspire to be organized, start saying, "I am now organized," rather than "I am going to be organized." As you use higher words, you change your mind, emotions, and the well-being of your physical body. Not only do you feel better, but you also begin to tune in to, to come into resonance with, other people who carry those same higher thoughts. This makes it easier for you to create events in your life that are more abundant, loving, joyful, and peaceful.

Watch when you use the words *should, have to,* and *must.* Do you frequently talk to yourself with these words? They often set up rebellion and create the opposite of their intent. Do you speak to yourself in a way that sounds like an angry parent, or do you have a loving voice within that permits you to flow with your own energy? When you catch yourself telling yourself you *have* to do something, explore whether you can change to something more permitting and gentle — a suggestion rather than a command.

Working with your mind is like taming a wild horse. At first your mind may rebel. As you try to learn to focus, your mind may sidetrack you, thinking of anything but what you want. As you bring your mind more completely under the guidance of your soul, you will realize that the thoughts you send out can work for or against you and other people.

Imagine that you are speaking of someone who is not present, criticizing this person for perceived faults. Realize that even though the person is not physically present, he or she can telepathically hear what you are saying. The person may not know it comes from you, and most likely will not know the exact words you are using, but he or she will feel less powerful and good about himself or herself. You will also pull to yourself criticism from other people who think of you.

You can raise the energy of the people around you or depress it by the thoughts you put into your mind. As you grow in your ability to sense energy, so do you grow in your ability to affect it. Thought involves very subtle energies. You can be obscure and unknown, or famous, and have just as much effect upon humanity. You may feel that you are very special, that you have an important mission, and yet feel you are not doing anything with your life that matches that feeling.

There is a universal belief that having a great mission means you must become famous. Many highly evolved souls with much important work to do choose to do it anonymously, without any outer-world recognition or fanfare. You cannot know the worth of the work you are doing here on earth if you are judging it by the standards of your personality, which looks at the form of it through other people's, or society's, standards. Only through the eyes of your soul can you know the impact of your life on humanity.

*By evolving yourself to the highest
level you can, you create a doorway for those
one step behind you to come through.*

Much of the great work done for humanity by very high beings is done in the telepathic arena, creating thoughts that have a high vibration. This usually does not involve public recognition. Every being that evolves to his or her next level makes it that much easier for those just one step behind to follow.

As you hold higher thoughts, learn your lessons, and radiate more love and peace, you are making a valuable contribution to humanity. You affect many people through those lines of thought that radiate out from you. Do not think that to have a great effect upon people you must be famous, that you must be on TV or the internet or write books. Some people are learning about certain fields of work and study so that, as they tap into the Universal Mind, they open that doorway for humanity. You make a contribution every time you create higher, wiser, and more loving thoughts.

There are those who hold a great vision and the energy of peace for the planet, so that when people think of peace they will be able to tune in to the energy of peace. These beings usually live solitary lives, virtually anonymous, often but not always living in isolated areas. The most important thing they do is hold the vision and experience of peace so all who desire it may find that energy telepathically available. Many of you are affecting the earth plane telepathically through your own personal broadcasts in ways you cannot know.

Your thoughts are like a magnet. The level of your thoughts determines not only what you attract but also what you affect.

As you think higher thoughts, you begin to connect with the higher forces in the Universe. As your mind creates an affinity with the higher planes, you begin to attract greater light and more harmony into your life. When you have thoughts of pain or fear, you attract like thoughts, and you may find it more difficult to reach upward, for you then connect with people who operate at a lower level.

Although your thoughts create reality, there is a veil between your thoughts and their ability to manifest, until you have reached a certain level of self-love and mental mastery. You may have wondered why your thoughts do not seem to always be able to create what you want.

For instance, you may be picturing your body thin, yet it is not responding. You are wondering why your thoughts are not manifesting a thinner reality. However, if you do not have many loving thoughts about your body, you would not want every thought about your body to manifest instantly. There will be a veil between the thought and the creation of it in that particular area until your thoughts about that area are brought up to a higher level. If you want to change this, you can learn to think about your body in more loving ways.

Notice whether you are finding fault with your body and having unloving thoughts about it, and if so change them to thoughts of acceptance. As you change all of your thoughts about your body into loving and accepting ones, it becomes possible to create the thinner body you are picturing, for your negative pictures are no longer present to hold you back.

You would not be able to handle it if every thought you had was created instantly in the physical world. Your life would change too quickly. Your home would be different from day to day. Your world could not function if everything changed with the rapidity of your thoughts. So you have created a veil that stands between you and the manifestation of your thoughts. You will be able to manifest your thoughts more quickly in the areas where they are loving and high.

If you have not mastered the unloving thoughts in an area, it would be too destructive to instantly manifest your thoughts in that area. If you are trying to get something and it is not coming, look at all of the thoughts you are having about that area of your life, and substitute thoughts of a higher quality for any negative thoughts you discover.

You have mental ties in every direction, in what has been called a "mental brotherhood" of humanity. One goal of your soul is to bring your mind into a higher, more loving vibration. To do this, you want to be open to receive thoughts from the higher levels of the Universe. Ask your soul, your guide, and the beings of light for inspiration, new ideas, and guidance. Attune yourself upward and you can experience many breakthrough ideas.

When you are idly thinking of other people, you draw in whatever feelings they have or whatever levels of thought they carry at that time. If they are in pain, you draw it in. That is why it is important, when you think of other people, to send them love, for when you are sending love or thinking of them with loving feelings you cannot pick up their broadcasts. If you notice people coming into your mind, radiate love to them and then let go of any thoughts of them. Do not dwell on their situation or on what is happening in their lives; do not make their reality your own.

You can *control your thoughts.*

You can train your mind to choose what you think and not allow thoughts to come up randomly and hold you in their grip. The thoughts that are in the trained mind are there by invitation and choice. You can turn away negative thoughts, repeatedly saying no to them. You can learn to substitute higher thoughts and words. You can learn to refrain from thinking those thoughts you do not want to think.

There are several techniques you can use to train your mind. One is to take an object such as a flower, crystal, or candle and spend a full minute focusing on it. If any other thoughts come into your mind, simply imagine them floating away as you continue to focus on the object. By not letting your mind wander, you are training it to think of what you are directing it to think of. Do this for fun. Note how long you can direct your mind to think about what you want it to. Explore whether you can increase the length of time you hold that focus steady, from one minute to five.

The next step is to look at the same object, then close your eyes and create it in your mind in perfect detail — the color, the texture, and the essence of the object. This helps you become more observant, and it helps train your mind to more accurately recognize what it knows through inner awareness, for often you see one thing and your mind tells you that you saw something else. It also develops your ability to hold an image steadily in your mind. Go back and forth, opening and closing your eyes, until you can "feel" the flower or object as if it were as real as an inner image as when viewed with your eyes.

This exercise will help you learn to make what you picture or imagine real in the outer world. If you determine that you will recognize all the beauty around you, and you begin to observe what is beautiful, holding those images clearly in your mind, you will soon become aware of beauty everywhere, even where you were not aware of it before.

A trained mind creates
emotional calm and inner peace
by focusing on higher ideals,
wisdom, and love.

Another way to train your mind is to simply observe for a period of time, one to five minutes, the flow of thoughts as they pass through your awareness. An untrained mind tends to find its attention caught by anything that comes its way. It is led by the attractions and impulses of the moment, by the cues from the world around and those things that come and go.

Watch the flow of your thoughts, for many thoughts are triggered by outer-directed stimuli such as phone calls, the internet, TV, and the people you are around. Thoughts of other people and telepathic connections can also trigger the mind. The goal is to learn to become inner directed, so that you decide what you want to think about rather than having your thoughts determined by what is happening around you. The untrained mind leads the emotions up and down according to the thoughts that march through.

Mental chatter needs to be calmed down before you can receive higher information. If you can stop that chatter for a second, feeling an inner sense of calm and a quiet mind, you create an opening for the higher vibration of your soul to reach you. Practice allowing higher thoughts into your mind by getting quiet and opening to your soul's light and wisdom.

Your mind is like a set of antennae extending outward in all directions. Thoughts come and go rapidly and are often triggered by sources outside of yourself, until you begin to bring them under the control and direction of your soul. Notice that when you suddenly think about something out of the blue, it is often because you are picking up thoughts from people you are connected to.

You need to stop responding automatically to your own thoughts and to the thoughts of others. You can begin to do so by turning your thoughts upward to your soul's light and love, by watching your inner dialogue and constantly substituting fine, high, and loving thoughts for any that are not as high as you would like.

> *You can change the energy between yourself and anyone by using positive words.*

Another exercise to train your mind can be done for fun with your friends and other people you connect with. Notice, as they talk to you, whether they are talking in past, present, or future time. Do they use words that uplift you, or do they use words and thoughts that strike chords in your lower self? Interject words in the conversation that are higher and lighter. You will feel your own brightness increasing and your own sense of joy growing larger as you speak words of encouragement.

If you would like to bring their energy up, say words that are high and loving and watch the change in their energy and yours. As you say these words, you keep from tuning in to the telepathic communication at lower levels from other people. You will begin to resonate with the thousands of minds that are thinking at these higher levels.

You will find yourself becoming stronger and clearer. If you hear someone saying something such as "The world is a frightening place," and you do not want that to be a part of your reality, mentally substitute different words, such as "The world is a joyful place."

You can use your mind to cancel out the negative words you hear from others, replacing them with higher, finer, and more loving thoughts. You will find that you make a different mirror, a reflection of a higher plane, available to others as well. Be aware that if you use this process, you may feel so light and joyful to other people that they will seek you out as popular company.

When you are with people, experiment with turning off your thoughts, even for a few moments. Do not react to, judge, or make any mental comments to yourself about what they are saying. Do not think about ways you can help them, do not think of responses, but listen with a silent mind. You will begin to pick up much beneath the surface of what they are saying, such as feelings, images, and pictures. Do this with a sense of play and discovery.

You can master your thoughts, your inner dialogue, and your personal broadcast. Over and over, decline negative thoughts that come into your mind. Substitute higher ones. Fix your mind on higher ideas no matter what is going on around you. Spend some time learning to hold a focus, taming your mind and harnessing it as your friend. As you do so, you will become a source of light and love for all around you.

PLAYSHEET

Chapter 13

Your Mind, Inner Dialogue, and Personal Broadcast

1. Think of the highest word or words you can for each letter in the alphabet.
2. Observe how you feel after thinking of high and positive words. A game to play while you are driving: look at car license plates and create high words out of the letters you see.
3. Find an object, such as a flower or crystal. Spend 30 seconds to a minute focusing on it. Notice whether you can concentrate on this object without being distracted by thoughts that come into your mind. Afterward, notice how hard or easy it was to keep your mind focused for that length of time.
4. Look at this same object and discover whether you can close your eyes and remember it exactly.

Wisdom: Being Your Higher Self

As you become aware of the energy around you, wisdom helps you understand it. You begin seeing that everything that happens to you happens to assist you in evolving and growing spiritually. As you come to know that the Universe creates all things for your highest good, your positive perspective creates a supportive and nurturing environment around you. You can then flow with the Universe rather than fight against it.

Wisdom is the ability to be conscious of what is happening around you, to be aware of a higher truth and express yourself with compassion. It makes the world around you friendly rather than hostile. Believing that everything is happening for your good renders negative energy harmless.

When you act with wisdom, you feel good inside. You know that you have stopped for a moment, taken the time to reflect, and reached upward for your direction. What you then create is from that higher space. You have demonstrated wisdom many times. Use your memories of the past to fill your consciousness with visions of yourself as a wise person, rather than remember the times you were not wise.

As you become more aware of energy, you will begin to sense people's thoughts and feelings to one degree or another. As you open to energy, you will begin to get more input and information from the Universe. Wisdom helps you to soften that information, to reinterpret the messages.

The way you view the world around you is the way you will experience it. Rather than thinking, "Everything is going against me" or "It is unfortunate that this happened," look at events from a higher perspective and realize that you can perceive everything happening to you as a good thing. This is the wisdom of your soul, for your soul is always trying to help you see your life from a higher perspective.

Feeling love rather than judgment
changes negative energy into
harmless energy.

Wisdom comes from the heart. The wise heart embraces others with a feeling of compassion for whatever stage they are at in their souls' evolution; it approaches them with a feeling of love and oneness rather than judgment. Wise people know that when they feel separate from those less evolved, they also separate themselves from those who are more evolved and, in doing so, delay their own journey upward. Through the eyes of love, all energy becomes more beautiful.

Wisdom is the ability to know what is important in your life and what is not, what things are distractions and what things are on your path and are the call of your soul. It is the ability to sort through all the data coming in and to select only those things that contribute to your sense of well-being. There may be something you want to accomplish and yet you never have the time because you keep getting distracted by housework, phone calls, or the demands of other people.

Wisdom is the ability to know which activities are truly serving your higher purpose and which are merely distractions from your path. You can make the people, thoughts, and events in your life positive, nurturing, and supportive. You can create a personal environment that is beneficial to you, rather than harmful.

Wisdom means understanding your mind and how it works. Your mind is a magnificent tool for learning. Because it wants to keep you motivated to learn more, it is never satisfied. No matter what you do, your mind always wants to move on to the next thing. You will feel unfulfilled and unsatisfied if you identify with your mind. As you identify with your true being, your soul, you will achieve feelings of inner contentment and peace. Your innermost Self, your true being, is the part of you that experiences your feelings and chooses what thoughts to have.

Rather than resisting or
getting rid of lower thoughts,
simply place thoughts of a
higher nature by their side.

Whatever you picture, you will get. Part of growth is choosing to picture higher things. Learn to identify "you" as the deeper part of your being, the part that chooses what thoughts to put in your mind, that selects emotions and reactions and desires.

As you evolve, you will work with your mind to hold high and positive thoughts. Even when beset by troubles, people with trained minds can stay away from the temptation of anxiety or anger by knowing that nothing stays in their minds that is not there by their choice and invitation.

When you are angry at someone, you can either express it or release it. Expressing anger, putting it out in the world verbally, always looking out to make sure no one takes advantage of you, telling people that they make you angry, will only attract more of what you are trying to avoid.

If you release anger, you no longer have it in you and you will not draw more to you. When you release those things that make you angry or sad or guilty, you no longer attract them to you. You can choose to release things without expressing anger, for you are a fully participating individual in everything that happens to you.

You may feel you do not have as much control as you would like over the things that happen to you, but you can control your response to them. You can choose how you want to react. You can select those responses that allow you to feel good. Rather than express anger, release it. Rather than express hatred, release it.

If you are having trouble releasing your reaction, turn upward to your soul and ask for help. Then another's anger or ill will cannot attach to you, for there is no place within you that it will stick to. Be generous with your forgiveness, for it is a response to anger that allows you to rise above it.

*Wisdom is being able
to discern which messages
to pay attention to and
which to release.*

When people speak to you in anger, saying unkind or untrue things, it is best to learn to forgive them. It is wise to learn not to respond to the negativity or fear in others. Keep your heart open and come from that loving, compassionate, and higher view. There are many who would speak of hard times, who blame others, and create bad feelings through their words and their anger. Learn not to respond with anger but to focus instead on other things.

Do not take offense, for offense taken is as bad as offense given. When you take offense, you contribute to negative energy between you and others. You create negative energy around you, and this attracts even more negative energy to you.

When you get offended, you close down your heart and turn away from your connection to your soul. Do not get offended when people speak from anger or fear, for it is coming from a lesser self within them. Learn to focus on their greater selves, for whatever you focus on and pay attention to is what you draw out in the people around you.

As you focus on the greatness in others, you will attract higher thoughts about yourself from other people. See them as doing the best they can. It is important not to react when people do not speak to you from their higher selves. Respond to them with compassion, as you would respond to a small child who does not know any better. Forgive them and let it go.

People cannot hurt you; only you can choose to hurt yourself by your response to them. This gives you the ultimate power to control the world you experience. If you are able to choose your response, you can choose to feel joy and peace and in this way change your world.

Learn to ignore the trivial and unimportant, so that others will hear you and pay attention when you speak of those things that are important. Learn to accept those things that do not matter, so that you will be able to pay attention to those that do. Train your focus and awareness to acknowledge beauty and harmony, so that you see the good and the wise. Turn your antennae in the direction of what is supportive and nurturing.

What is loving to the self is ultimately loving to others as well.

Learn to know the difference between your wishes and the wishes of others. You can acquire the ability to choose what is right for you by checking in with your higher self. If you find a feeling of distress or resistance, take time to look deeper. What is right for you will also be right for other people. Have you ever forced yourself to go somewhere with someone because you felt obligated, only to discover the other person did not really want to go there either? Have you ever canceled an appointment and found that the other person was getting ready to call you to do the same?

Allow yourself to choose which energies you want to feel and be a part of and which energies you simply want to release. You may be having many experiences right now in which others want something from you, are disappointed in you, or are accusing you of not living up to what they expect. Wisdom is learning what is yours — your thoughts, your expectations — and what is another person's.

How do you tell what energy is yours and what is others'? Often you cannot tell until you "wear" their energy. For instance, when you live with a person, and he or she feels strongly about a moral issue, you may find yourself taking the same view. Then, when you separate, you discover that you feel differently about that issue. You have "worn" someone else's beliefs for a while. You may discover that you love to think the way someone else does, or you may find out that you do not.

From time to time in the process of growth, you will bring other people's energy into your life; you will try living by their rules, principles, and values to discover if they are yours. You may choose to keep those that agree with you. It will be your opportunity for growth to let go of those that do not.

Do not feel guilty if you find yourself rejecting another's views or beliefs, even when those beliefs seem to be moral or to fit with what people call "right." Only you can know what is right for yourself. It is the same with all energy you perceive in the world; if certain energy does not work for you, then you do not need to keep it.

Wisdom is the ability to know when to act and when not to.

Wisdom is not the mind, although it includes the mind. Your mind gathers all the facts and tries to make decisions based upon known data. Wisdom comes from combining what you intuitively know with what you intellectually know. It helps you know which impulses come from your lower nature and which come from your higher self.

Often your mind presents you with many ideas. More opportunities may come to you than you can possibly act upon. Do not make yourself wrong if you cannot bring yourself to act upon what seems to be a golden opportunity. Follow that deeper note of understanding that says in a whisper, "Wait." Or, if your mind is telling you to wait but that inner voice says to act, take a leap of faith, dare to take a risk; then do so.

You might ask how great masters would demonstrate wisdom. They would know when to be strict and stern, and when to be loving and generous. Not always is it wise to give people what they think they need. Small children may think they need an unlimited supply of candy to be happy; you, with a higher view, can see that good nutrition will serve them better in the long run. Sometimes it is necessary to hold a higher vision for others and assist them in recognizing it themselves, rather than giving them what they are asking for. You may even need to deny them something they think they need.

People who have a great deal of money have discovered that giving people money does not solve all their problems; in fact, it often creates more trouble. You may have enough money to lend relatives in need, but your wise self knows that they have created a lack of money to learn lessons that will assist them in becoming more abundant in the future. You may be of more assistance to them by helping them discover their higher purpose and encouraging them to do what they love than by giving them money, which will last a short while but will not help in the long run. Indeed, when they run out of money, you and they are in the same spot.

Wisdom is knowing how to teach people to fish, rather than giving them fish. It is knowing when to help and when not to. For instance, when watching children learn a new skill, it is tempting to jump in and show them how to do it better. Yet, they cannot learn unless they try it themselves, however good or bad the effort. You must, in your wisdom, stand by quietly and let them learn by trial and error. It is the same with friends and loved ones in your life.

Often, the most loving thing you can do for people is to stand by while they learn their lessons. If you come in and act as their savior, you may take away the lessons and growth they were getting out of that situation. Then they will have to create it all over again. You can assist them more by focusing on the light within them and by helping them recognize what they are learning from the situation. It may feel hard to be wise, for often it is easier to jump in and rescue people than to stand by and watch them go through difficult and sometimes painful lessons.

> *It is important
> to experience compassion
> rather than sympathy.*

Sympathy is feeling sorry for others, seeing that what is happening to them is negative or bad. Compassion is both realizing that what is happening to them is for their growth and assisting them in recognizing that for themselves. Compassion reframes an experience they may perceive as unfortunate or bad into something they can understand.

Realize that when you feel sympathy for people, you begin to vibrate with them and take their lower energy into yourself. When you offer compassion, you do not bring in their negativity.

Being firm with people may not be easy. However, doing so can be a greater gift than being too accommodating. You may have people you have given and given to who do not seem to appreciate what you do, or to grow and change their lives in response to all the advice and assistance you have given them. If your help is doing no apparent good, it is time to put your energy elsewhere. You may risk not being liked in the short run, but in the long run you will gain from following this higher wisdom.

One of the greatest gifts you give others is precise, accurate, and compassionate communication of the truth. It takes a great deal of wisdom to know what to say and when to say it. If you are in doubt about saying something to people, go within before you speak. If it feels like your communication will serve them in their growth, then say it. If it feels like it will fall on deaf ears or they will resist it, keep it to yourself.

If you are speaking out of a desire for personal gain, to get them to do something you want them to do, it is better to remain silent. Personal gain cannot be the motivation if you are truly to help. There is power in silence, and there is power in communication given at the right time.

Before you speak, ask yourself, "Does this communication serve people's highest vision?" If it does, then you are speaking with wisdom. A wise person chooses words with precision when speaking. Before communicating to others, a wise person asks, "How does what I say serve their growth?" If it does not serve them in any way, it is not said. Whenever you put out high and wise energy, you draw it back to yourself.

Recognize the level of the soul you are with. Do not expect calculus from a second grader. Be gentle with those around you. Any negative energy sent your way is caused by their fear; you do not need to react with fear yourself.

Can you imagine what it would be like if you were only as open and loving as the people around you? The challenge is to use your innate wisdom to see all situations from a higher perspective, to release the energy you do not want, and to act from your own center of love and compassion, regardless of the level of love in the people around you.

Be the leader. Dare to be wise! Dare to be the one who is the most loving, compassionate, open, and vulnerable. Set the example; do not wait for others to be open and wise first. You will soon discover the power of one open, wise, and loving person to transform the entire world around him or her.

PLAYSHEET

Chapter 14

Wisdom: Being Your Higher Self

1. Sit quietly and relax. Think about the day and week ahead. Ask your soul to assist you in recognizing which of the things you are planning to do are truly important and which ones are merely distractions that you could eliminate.

2. Ask your soul to show you the most important thing you could accomplish today. Make the decision that you will do it.

3. Is there anything you plan to do in the next day or week that is an obligation or another's wish for you, rather than your own? Ask your soul to assist you in letting go of doing this.

4. Think of someone in your life who wants something from you that you do not feel right about giving. Get quiet and bring in your wise higher self. Is there anything you could give, other than what that person thinks he or she needs, that would truly serve him or her?

Telepathy: Understanding Nonverbal Communication

There are two basic forms of communication, verbal and telepathic, or nonverbal. Each of you has experienced telepathy. You constantly receive emotional or mental telepathic messages from your loved ones, your friends, and the world around you. You are telepathically connected to not only people you know now but also people you will know and those whom you have known. You might think of these telepathic connections as invisible as the radio waves that are all about you. They do exist, and you can and are receiving them.

You can learn to turn down the volume, sever the ties, monitor what comes in and goes out, and transform negative energy into positive energy. The loudest broadcast you receive is from those you love, whom you open your heart to; and the faintest whispers usually come from those you knew years ago and from casual or distant friends. It is important to know how to control the volume, the frequency, and how you receive these messages, emotionally or mentally, for the quality of your telepathic connections determines whether your bonds will be positive and help you or hinder you.

Be aware of the thought forms in your community.

You are telepathically part of a larger community consisting of your neighborhood and your town. Communities have certain thought forms that are unique to them, and those thoughts are very real. Each community is a pocket of energy. You pick up the messages of your community from everywhere — restaurants, bookstores, grocery stores, and the internet, even from the cars you drive past.

When you sit and eat in a restaurant, you can pick up the feelings and thoughts of the people around you. All of you can pick up the thought forms of your community and the thoughts and feelings of your neighbors. Telepathic reception is stronger the closer you physically are to people.

Do you find that you feel better in a place other than where you live? Do you find that you like being one place and dislike being somewhere else? You may not be compatible with the thought forms of the neighborhood and the community you are in. Look at your neighbors, their belief systems and reality, and you will begin to get an idea of the thought forms you live around.

The telepathic influences of those closest to you — loved ones and friends — are even stronger. Everyone is a telepathic sender and receiver to some degree. All communication comes first from the telepathic sending and receiving of it. It is often followed by words, but underneath the words people speak are many nuances of feelings and pictures that are being transmitted and received telepathically.

Your mind is like a TV set with many channels. Coming in on one station, for instance, could be your husband, wife, or partner. You may have a separate station for each friend. Many thousands of messages swirl around you all day. You can learn to choose which ones you will pick up and respond to.

Are you a victim of all those telepathic messages? Are you fated to have low energy because those around you have low energy? It depends upon your ability to turn the dial and select what you bring into yourself. Most of you experience telepathy on an emotional level, bringing in other people's emotions. It is far better to receive messages through your higher centers. You tend to bring in other people's feelings and think they are yours if you receive information emotionally. That is how many of you lose a sense of who you are.

Imagine you are sitting in an apartment, and the neighbors on one side have a radio playing loud rock and roll. The neighbors on the other side of you are playing very loud classical music. Your own TV is going in one room of your apartment, and you have a radio playing in another. Neighbors above and below you are playing completely different music, and you also hear loud voices coming from all the various apartments. Imagine how hard it would be to get in touch with your own energy with all that noise going on. That is what most of you experience all day long. It is happening at a subconscious level, but the telepathic noise and chatter is there.

You can learn to decipher the messages, choosing which ones you want to hear and accept and which ones you want to ignore. You can learn to stop receiving them. You can learn how to use the telepathic messages around you for your and others' highest good.

Imagine walking into a room and finding that the person you have come to see is nervous and fearful. Suddenly you find yourself more worried about your life and more tense about things in general. Most of you experience this frequently without even realizing you are picking up emotional telepathic energy. You may simply think, "I am really jumpy." You may even be picking up messages on your way to places.

Have you ever noticed, as you go to see someone, that as you get closer you become very happy, or tired and unhappy, or anxious? All of these are examples of picking up emotional messages from others. The feelings seem like your own, until you learn to recognize them as coming from others.

You cannot know
what you are picking up telepathically
until you know your own energy.

To become aware of your own energy, focus on yourself as you wake up in the morning. You feel different each morning, have different issues on your mind — people you are going to see, new things that will come up for you that day.

As you wake up, you have not yet begun picking up the telepathic transmissions from people you are going to see, and you are the most aware of who you are. Ask, "How do I feel?" You may find you are waking up tense or elated and happy. Focusing on your feelings as you wake up establishes a reference point you can use all day. If you wake up tense, take time to center yourself and to feel peaceful before you go out into the world, because you will attract thoughts, situations, and circumstances that mirror your feelings.

You may know that in the evening you are going to see someone, a loved one or a friend. You may be thinking of something you are going to do, or thinking of work you are doing on a project. You may be thinking about your job, family, or friends. As you telepathically tune in to those people you will be associating with, you begin to pull in their energy. If you first experience your own feelings, then you can be aware of any changes in yourself when you think about or are around other people.

As you think of other people, note any changes in your energy. For instance, you wake up happy, but as you think about going to work and dealing with a coworker, you begin to feel anxious or irritated. If you did not remember that you woke up feeling good, you might think that these feelings are yours. Having recognized how you felt as you woke up, you can see that you picked up your coworker's tension and irritability as you thought about him or her.

If you wonder how people feel about you, ask yourself how you feel when you think of them. If you are not aware of how you felt when you woke up, or before you thought of them, you will not be able to experience the difference in yourself when you think of them. If you think about them and become sad, or feel they do not respect you or want to be with you, notice how those feelings compare to what you were feeling before you started thinking of them. You will then know, at a feeling level, how people are responding to you.

People are aware of your nonverbal communication with them at some level. If you are fighting telepathically with some people, saying to them, "I do not want you to treat me this way, I will not take it anymore, I will not do this or that," they are aware of what you are sending them and you may experience more struggle and resistance from them. They are not picking up your precise words.

People usually pick up your message only as a feeling from you, depending upon their ability to receive; they will pick it up emotionally and work with it on that level. Your message will feel bad to them; and when they tune in to you, they will most probably have an urge to pull away. If you are thinking intently about people who do not want to be aware of you, or other people are thinking of you and you do not want them to, you and they always have the power to stop receiving unwanted thoughts.

If you are spending hours reflecting on certain people, are they spending time thinking about you? You have the ability to know. If, when you think of them, you feel a sense of resistance or irritation from them, then they are not thinking of you and they find your thoughts an intrusion. Or they may be in an irritable mood, and you are feeling their energy. If, on the other hand, you find it delightful to think about them or have a warm feeling in your heart, then they are welcoming you to join them on the telepathic level.

You have the ability to sense what others are thinking.

The first step is to get into a centered, relaxed feeling. You cannot clearly sense energy through intense emotions. If you want to know what another person is thinking, relax and calm yourself and let your mind be as silent as possible. You may want to imagine you are in the other person's shoes, looking at yourself. Almost always, the underlying feeling you have when you think of others is the feeling they have when they think of you. If you are going back and forth about how you feel about them, then they are probably doing the same about you. The particular issues may not be identical, but the underlying feeling is something you can learn to trust.

If someone has not called you, for instance, and you have been waiting for him or her to connect with you, look at your own thoughts and feelings, for others pick up your thoughts and feelings when they think of you. If you have said in your mind, "I really do not like the way you are treating me and I do not want you in my life," that may be why the person stopped calling you.

Be aware that people do receive your telepathic messages, especially in a close relationship. When you send out firm decisions, people immediately pick them up. You can always feel when people are inviting you to join them telepathically. It is easy and pleasant to link with them mentally. You can send them messages and feel their presence without a heavy feeling in your heart. You can be aware of them without feeling sad, depressed, or pushed away.

When you send out emotional messages, you affect other people. What you broadcast is picked up by those who love and care about you. Humanity is opening telepathically.

> *You can gain control*
> *over the telepathic messages*
> *you send and receive.*

Everyone is, to some degree, affected by others telepathically. Monitor your energy constantly throughout the day. After a while you will get used to checking your emotional states and thoughts often. At least once when you are with someone, pay attention to how you feel. Do you feel better or worse? Do you suddenly feel more troubled, more anxious, or happier?

Knowing what you feel like, you can learn to recognize when others are affecting you. You will learn only through practice; there is no shortcut.

Many of you are looking for ways to connect with your higher selves by developing your ability to tune in to your inner guidance. Emotional messages of others and your own thought patterns can interfere with your ability to receive this guidance. Once you have learned to tune in to and monitor your feelings, you will have a clearer sense of how you pick up energy from other people emotionally and mentally.

If you want a deep,
loving relationship with another,
first become aware of who you are.

People often receive telepathic messages in their emotional center from those who love them and those they love. Many people would like a deep meaningful connection, that kind of relationship in which two people are so linked that each anticipates what the other wants and needs. A fear of that deep bond, however, keeps many people from it. If you are not centered and aware of who you are, you cannot begin to join with another at that deeper level without losing yourself.

Are you happy today? Are you sad? For a moment, remember when you woke up this morning. Go all the way back and ask how you felt. Picture yourself moving through the day. Recapture some of your emotions; take a look at who you were with and notice your changing emotional energy. Were you affected by other people you were with or thought about?

It is important to understand your emotional reception of energy, because as a child you often felt the emotions of others as if they were your own, and you were not taught how to stop, change, or transmute them. Most of you went through childhoods in which you did not know who you were. You were so open telepathically to the wishes, wants, and demands of others that you often thought what they wanted was what you wanted. As a result, many of you are confused about your identity. You are usually very open telepathically if you desire to help, counsel, or support others, professionally or just as friends.

Many of you grew up as very sensitive children, aware of how people around you were feeling, and bombarded with messages from all around. There are many unique challenges associated with growing up as an intuitive, sensitive person. You may have experienced great sensitivity, caring for other people's feelings almost more than your own, sensing another person's pain as if it was your pain. You tried to protect others from feeling pain, loving others at a level you often did not find returned.

Growing up telepathically sensitive can mean hearing double messages from your parents and others — "No, I am fine today, dear," when you sense sadness and tension. It can mean wondering how people can be cruel when you yourself cannot bear to hurt anyone because you feel the pain in another. It leaves you wondering if people are insensitive and cold, or if you are the only one who can perceive certain things around you.

For some of you it meant feeling you were somehow different from others. You may have felt as a child that you did not fit in, and school, with its social life, was often hard. On

174 Personal Power through Awareness

the other hand, some of you may have used your sensitivity to fit right in, be successful, and get what you wanted.

Many people are going through the problems associated with being telepathic today. It is important to understand that part of your inability to know who you are comes from the telepathic abilities that exist within you. Many of you have had experiences with telepathy, perhaps more than you would even want.

The example I gave earlier of all the radio stations and all the TVs playing at once is how most of you likely had to deal with your childhood. You were picking up demands and telepathic messages from many people, and most of you tried hard to please. You could see that it was easier to give people what they wanted, though some of you rebelled and did the opposite if the demands went too much against who you were, or if it appeared that certain people would never be satisfied. Many of you used anger and rebellion to block the control other people tried to exert over you.

Telepathy is a problem when it is not understood, and a gift and a responsibility when it is.

If you are telepathic, you can send messages as well as receive them. You have a responsibility to others in what you send out. Most of you receive and send from the emotional center, but you can also send with words, which moves your communication to the mental level.

Almost everyone experiences emotional telepathy, but fewer experience mental telepathy. While it is not something that makes you better or superior to others, telepathy can be a problem, as well as a gift, unless you learn about it. Being mentally telepathic, you are able to pick up messages and send them out. Do you understand how you can affect others with this gift?

You have certain ways of thinking, patterns of thought that occur throughout the day. Have you noticed when you are walking or riding in a car that your mind automatically falls into certain patterns, reflecting perhaps on mundane things, your or a friend's problems, or something else that you think of when you have nothing better to do?

You have a responsibility to move these thoughts to a higher energy level, for others receive and can be affected by them. To change these thought habits will require a commitment to change and then a conscious effort to bring them up to a higher level when you recognize their presence.

It is important to learn to focus your mind on what you choose, thinking of higher ideals rather than the mundane. It does not matter that the things you do seem unimportant or minor; it is not the kind of work you do but the way in which you do it and how you think about it that determines your evolution. Practice controlling your thoughts of things that seem unimportant, and you will be prepared to watch your thoughts on the larger and more important things.

You may find yourself conversing with people in your mind, talking to them and going back and forth. You may find yourself discussing things with them as if you truly have a conversation going on. Whatever you are sending out in words is being received by the other person. This is mental rather than emotional telepathy.

Most people do not have the ability to receive words as clearly as you are sending them; most people receive your telepathic thoughts as feelings. Others may find themselves carrying on a mental debate with you. You may notice that the next time you get together it is as if you start verbally where you left off mentally.

If you are telepathic, you have a responsibility. You cannot pretend you do not know what is happening between you and another person. You do know at a deep level, and you can learn to bring that knowing to the light of consciousness. You are responsible for what you send out. When you send anger, you are sending it out to all those you know. You then begin to resonate with those people who are angry and you bring their broadcasts into yourself.

You may think that you are sending your anger just to the person you are mad at, but be aware that on the telepathic level it goes out to the world. When you are loving and peaceful, you send that energy out to others to come into harmony with if they choose.

When you think of others,
they receive energy from you.

I have been asked many times, "When I think of people, does that mean they are thinking of me? Who thought of whom first?" It is a very interesting question, and one that has no simple answer.

If you think of people spontaneously, people you do not think of often, and out of the blue you get a strong thought or picture of them, then they are probably thinking of you at the same time or have thought of you very recently. If you have an ongoing relationship with someone, and you spend a great deal of time thinking about the person — asking mental questions, talking to or debating with him or her — the person may or may not be thinking of you at the same time.

Imagine you are making and sending someone a prerecorded message as you think of him or her. You do not need to connect at the same instant. The person receives your message while in a state of receptivity. People may not hear your messages as clearly as you are sending them, but they will get them in some way.

Say you are arguing with someone, telling him or her in your mind you do not like the way you are being treated. If the person is highly empathic (able to receive), your message will likely be heard and you will be aware of an ongoing debate. If the person is not developed telepathically, your thoughts may be received only as a feeling of resentment or anger, and the person may feel puzzled or angry at what is happening. He or she may not get the transmission the instant you send it but will play it back like a recorded message later while he or she is in a receiving state — such as a time of silence, reflectiveness, dreaminess, meditation, or any state of quietness of mind.

You can compare sending out messages in your mind to dialing a phone. Nobody can answer you while you are dialing the phone. Only after you are finished dialing can you connect with them. When you are thinking of another, you are sending out a message. When you are listening, you are not sending.

You may have noticed that when you are sitting around wanting someone to call, no one calls; but five or six hours later, suddenly everyone is calling you. You may be busy and not even thinking of them anymore. It is because when you send out inner messages people usually (although not always) require time to receive and act upon them. Just as people do not answer their phone when they are busy, so does it take a while for people to be silent enough to hear your message. If they are silent, perhaps meditating or daydreaming when you are sending out your message, they may get it instantaneously and may even act upon it quickly.

When you are deeply connected with and thinking of people, you put your mental communications on a "mental recording" that is available for them to play when and if they choose. When it comes to receiving messages from others, most of you are not aware that you have the choice of playing them, stopping and starting them, and choosing only those segments you want to hear. You may allow whole recordings to play, which can create stress if the recordings are not good ones.

How can you learn to tune in to mental recordings and play them when you want? When you think of people, you turn on the recorder and allow their communications to come through to you. You have the ability to turn these off at any time, either by not thinking of these people or by sending them positive, loving images, for when you are sending images you cannot receive their thoughts and feelings.

If you do not want to hear any recording a person may have transmitted to you, simply do not think about him or her. You have the ability to stop thinking of someone by finding things that are interesting and joyful to think of instead. You can send anyone high, loving thoughts and pictures of their inner beauty and strength whenever they come into your mind, and you will be less affected by their messages.

It is energizing and fun
to change your thinking habits and
experience new, higher thoughts.

When you are driving your car, thinking of your errands for the day and your responsibilities, you can also make a conscious effort to think of your higher purpose, your path, and what you can contribute to the world. You can think of those qualities you want to bring into your life — unconditional love, inner peace, and wisdom.

You may have to consciously choose these thoughts and train your mind over and over to think of these things rather than your normal thoughts. You may stay at a high level for only a few seconds at first, until your mind gets used to thinking about higher ideals and principles. As you find more enlightened topics to think about, you will shut off your old thinking patterns and the messages that come into your awareness from lower levels.

You can use the same technique to turn off the inner recorder. If you do not wish to receive messages from certain people, then do not tune in to them. Find things to occupy your mind that energize you and bring you joy, and in so doing you will slowly and surely disconnect from their communications. Another option is to imagine that you are receiving their messages as voicemails, and that you simply delete their messages without listening to them.

How can you listen only to the part of the message you want to hear? Take, for example, a case in which you find you get depressed thinking of someone. You get a heavy feeling or perhaps feel drained when thoughts of him or her come into your mind. You may feel sorry for this person and wish that he or she would get his or her life together. You may be going through a difficult time in your relationship and find it depresses you to think about this person.

To hear only the good part of people's inner messages, make a conscious effort to center yourself when you think about them. If you drift into thinking of someone, you open yourself to any messages from this person that come through.

However, if you orient yourself before you think of someone, focusing on your own energy, feeling relaxed, calm, and confident, you can bring in the more loving message the person's soul is sending you.

If you send your calmness, you can control what portions of others' communications come to you, rather than receiving their problems. In the case of a person who is draining you, you can choose consciously to send thoughts such as "I see you as a loving and high being. I want to speak from my soul-self to yours, and I will now open myself to listening to you." If you do not like the feeling of what comes back, you can either shut off your reception of it or send healing to this person.

To send energy that is healing and helpful to people, experience your love and compassion for them. Imagine them getting their lives together in whatever way is appropriate. See their greatness and soul-beauty. Sending loving, appreciative thoughts will also improve the quality of your telepathic messages. If every time you think of someone you also send a loving, supportive thought, you will find a tremendous difference in the messages that come back to you.

*There are ways to
stop thinking of a person,
if that is your desire.*

Consciously focus on things that are fun and joyful to think about. Take the time to develop some joyful images or fantasies and have them ready whenever the other person pops into your mind. You must intend to stop thoughts of him or her, or they will keep coming back. It is a wonderful opportunity to train your mind.

You connect telepathically most often with those you have opened your heart to. It is a challenge to turn off your thoughts when a bond exists at the heart level. If you do not wish to go around hearing the inner messages that have been sent to you, be aware that every time you allow yourself to think of someone, you are letting yourself receive whatever has been sent out to you. You are also open to receiving whatever feelings the other person is experiencing. If you send a thought of love, you will not bring the other person's energy into your awareness.

If you want something from someone and you push the person telepathically to give it to you, you will push him or her away. Sometimes the more a person pulls away from you, the more likely you are to push even harder to get through. If someone demands something from you that you do not want to give, you feel pushed and your natural reaction is to pull away. If you create space within yourself by pulling back and concentrating on your own life and purpose, you will probably find the other person desiring to connect with you.

If you want something from people, if you want them to think of you, be with you, or give you attention, the way to get it is by withdrawing your attention from them. Most of you do the opposite — you think of someone constantly; you put all your energy into them, and the results are exactly the opposite of what you want. You bombard that person with your messages and your energy, which is always around them. Why should they seek out your company when you are always with them every time their mind relaxes?

If you want attention from someone, make an effort to stop thinking of him or her and get on with your own life. Focus on something else every time you begin to think of the person or situation, or send light and see the person and related situation dissolving in your mind. Do not check in constantly to see if it is working (is he or she paying attention now?), because when you do that you are sending the person energy. You must come to the point where you are so involved with your life and work that there is truly a vacuum. When he or she senses you, there is nothing there. Then the person will be drawn to you, if it is his or her purpose to connect with you.

Many of you think that when you want something, and you picture somebody giving it to you, you will get it. It usually works in just the opposite way — you create resistance.

If you want something from
somebody, picture a time
in which you gave that
same thing to someone else.

For instance, if you have guests staying with you and you want them to help with the housework, remember a time you offered to do housework for people you were staying with. If you want someone to be kinder to you, picture times when you were kind to someone else. This does not guarantee that they will respond in any particular way; you cannot manipulate other people with these thoughts. However, you open the space for them to more likely respond in the way you would like.

There is a big difference between picturing someone doing something for you and picturing a time when you did that same thing for someone else. Imagine wanting something from somebody and asking for it over and over, either verbally or in your mind. Most people respond by drawing away.

If instead you fill your mind with thoughts of the times you offered those same things, every time the person thinks of you he or she will pick up the pictures with which you are surrounding yourself. As this person tunes in to your pictures, he or she will begin to think of doing the things you are remembering doing for other people.

How do you handle people who are draining you? First of all, be aware that they could not drain you if you did not give them permission, in some way, to do so. You may say, "I do not want them to drain me," but you are at some level allowing them to do so. If you do not set your own limits and boundaries, they will not set any either.

You must say very clearly, for instance, "I will not be drained by these people; I will not accept responsibility for their lives," and then you will not be drained. If you do not take responsibility for other people's well-being, then they can no longer take your energy. You can, however, send them thoughts of love and peace, which will help them.

Being drained is not caused by telepathic connections as much as by your own beliefs and personality, the decisions you have made about what rights you have and do not have with the people in your life. You can learn to be unaffected by people who make demands of you. If you feel you owe it to them to hear their complaints, to be there for them even though you do not want to, you will continue to feel drained by them. You may be saying, "There is no way I can disconnect from them." And yet there is, by first affirming to yourself that you absolutely have the right to live your own life.

If there are people you must be physically around, such as in your home or office, you can change the energy between you by focusing on whatever good you can recognize in them. You can transmit love, forgiveness, and acceptance. You can learn to stay out of judgment, fear, or anger around this person. Ask to see all that you are learning and why you drew these kinds of people into your life. Refuse to let them draw you into their negativity, and use this as an opportunity to learn how to stay balanced and centered in your own energy, no matter who you are around.

The degree to which you feel responsible for other people's happiness is the degree to which they can pull on you and take from you. They can use guilt and manipulation only because you allow them to by believing you owe them something. If you turn over the responsibility for their lives to them, you will not feel so uncomfortable.

You can say to yourself, "Only they can make themselves powerful, create good feelings, and give to themselves," and then you will no longer feel exhausted by communication with them. They can pull on you only when you feel that they can, when you allow them to take from you because you feel you do not deserve to have people leave you alone.

One person asked me about a neighbor who acted angry and cold and was not responding to the love and good thoughts she was sending him. She wondered what to do with his negative energy. If you are sending people love over and over and they seem to be responding with negative energy or none at all, they may not wish to have you send them energy and love.

In this case, the woman needed to withdraw her energy from her neighbor. When she did so, he felt free to seek her out. He had been so filled with her energy that he had resisted it; it was far more love than he could handle. In fact, she stopped sending him any thoughts. Within a month, when he saw her outside gardening, he went to the fence between their properties to ask if there was anything he could help her with.

You can calm
your emotions by saying
inspiring, loving words
over and over.

What if you experience a lot of pain when you think of someone, or you get an emotional knot that is overwhelming and seems to block out your ability to think loving thoughts? At times, the only way to calm emotions is to turn up the volume of your mind. You can learn to say high words to yourself whether you believe in them or not. You are not drowning out the voice of pain; you are instead turning up the volume of your higher self.

Do not make the part of you that is in pain wrong or bad, for that increases its power over you. If it is saying, "This is not working; everything is going wrong; this person has deserted me or dislikes me," say high and positive statements over and over in your mind. Even if you cannot focus on the words, and you find your mind going in and out of higher thoughts, persist, because the mind can absolutely rule the emotions.

You have been given the gift of thought to help you gain mastery over your lower self. Thoughts can assist in your personal transformation. Your mind is a marvelous instrument capable of bringing the light of wisdom where there is ignorance and darkness.

If you feel overwhelmed by your emotions, begin writing affirmations such as "The Universe is working in perfect harmony. Everything happens for my higher good. I now see a Universe of beauty and perfection." Think these things; say them over and over. Flood your mind with a voice that says,

"Things are positive; things are working in my favor; all is in good order."

The more you fill your mind with positive thoughts, the more you will turn down the volume of negative thoughts that can trigger strong emotional responses. Affirm spiritual truths and the principles of the soul, such as harmony, balance, and peace. If you keep saying high words, the very vibration of them will begin to calm your emotions. It requires discipline and practice. There are no easy solutions. If you truly intend to live at a higher level of consciousness, you can; and then the results you want will follow.

Most importantly, ask your soul to assist you in calming your emotions. Your soul is always with you, and it is the light that shines on both your emotions and your mind, lifting you out of the denser realms into the light and joy of the higher realms.

PLAYSHEET

.Chapter 15

Telepathy: Understanding Nonverbal Communication

1. Think about when you woke up this morning. How did you feel? What things about the day were on your mind?

2. Who did you see or talk to today? How did your energy change before, during, and after you saw them? Can you find instances in which you took their energy into yourself? Make a written or mental list of whoever you saw and how you felt.

3. Take any feelings or thoughts you did not like when you were with a specific individual and imagine yourself dissolving those emotions and thoughts in your soul's light. Breathe deeply and feel yourself returning to a balanced, centered feeling.

Receiving Guidance
from the Higher Realms

You can learn to receive information from the higher realms of the Universe. Just as there are telepathic broadcasts from people, there are many higher broadcasts you can tune in to. High levels of guidance and information are available at any time. Just as you cannot see or touch a radio wave, you cannot be aware of or receive these broadcasts unless you have the will and intent to do so and practice what you have learned about sensing energy.

What are these broadcasts? There are different levels of information: some involve science, some involve business, teachings of all kinds, or visions of peace and love. All knowledge known and yet to be known is available to you when you attune yourself to the Universal Mind, the collective whole of knowledge that exists outside of time and space.

Many great scientists have tapped into this level for their scientific inventions. Many new discoveries, ideas, and concepts come from attunement with the Universal Mind. You can bring in information to aid you with your business, increase your creativity, or help you become prosperous. Those of you who think of planetary peace and strive to bring peace into your own lives can come into harmony with the broadcast of peace that is always available.

A broadcast of healing is available at all times. Its essence is love, compassion, and peace. When you need help, guidance, or love, it is always available as a broadcast you can tune in to in order to raise your energy and heal whatever needs love. Healers and those in counseling professions often draw from this level in the course of their work; everyone can tune in to it. As you attune yourself to this level, you feel as if you know what to do or say with a certainty that comes from a level beyond your conscious knowledge.

True healing involves
compassion and love
for both yourself and others.

If you are using your hands in bodywork, if you are bringing through healing information or energy, if you are helping people through your voice, thoughts, or words, you are often drawing from this Universal broadcast. As you help others to grow, heal, and evolve spiritually, you are tapping into this Universal broadcast of healing and love, as it is the source of the healing you offer others.

Guidance is also available from many high masters and spirit teachers, both those physically present on the earth and those who are in other realms. Many high souls who are no longer living are holding a focus of peace and love for humanity and are available for personal guidance. You call them guides, for they are there to help hold a high vision for humanity and any person who calls upon them. All of you have a guide, whether you are aware of your guide or not. There are many different ways in which your guide can send you information. Any answers you seek, any information you want, is always there.

Guides can help you become aware of your ability to reach higher planes of knowledge and experience, to discover your own wisdom and your soul's constant guidance. A guide will never take away your lessons, but will help you become aware of what you are learning so that you may move through your growth lessons more easily. When asked, a guide can show you an expanded view of any situation, presenting a perspective that allows you to understand what is happening and to act in more loving and compassionate ways. When you view any situation through this wise, expanded perspective, it is possible to let go of pain and embrace yourself as a warm and loving person.

> *All you need to do
> to receive guidance is to
> ask for it and then listen.*

You can tune in to any of these levels of guidance and information if you have the will and intent to do so. What is will and intent? You may have a picture of your will as that part of you that says, "I will force myself to do this or that."

Right use of will is when you love doing something so much that you do it without having to will it or push yourself. You have seen the results when you love to do something, and you have seen what happens when you really do not want to do something but force yourself to do it anyway. You do not produce good results when you make yourself do something or when you have a lot of indecision about doing it.

Will is a clear focus that you direct toward something you love. The less your focus is diluted by fears, doubts, and resistance, the more it becomes like a laser beam, directing you to where you want to go, gaining you a greater ability to draw something to you.

Some of you may say you want certain things, think of them often, and then wonder why you do not get them. The less certain you are about getting what you want, the longer it takes to get it. When you are clear and your will is focused, you bring what you want to you.

Those of you who are healers, teachers, or counselors have a great deal of motivation, intent, and desire that makes your healing and guidance possible. Helping others may be something you consciously chose or something you seemed to "fall into," but to become skilled and good you have had to focus a great deal of your intent and will on it. Will is the dial that tunes you in to the right station. There is no magical formula for being a healer with your hands, mind, or words or for being a spiritual channel.

If you aspire to be anything — a writer, actress, athlete, channel, good parent, successful businessperson — you need only have the intent to do this and willingness to act on your inner guidance. The broadcast from the higher levels of the Universe and from your soul directs you to your highest path. That broadcast is always available to anyone who wants and asks for it. Your will and intention to be something or do something begins to automatically tune you in to the Universal broadcast that is appropriate for you.

Many of you would like to be more directly involved in helping people. You may be in jobs that do not feel aligned with your purpose. You may wonder if you should be doing something else, if there is some mission you should be fulfilling even though you do not know what it is. The fact that you are thinking these things is an indication that you are healers, teachers, or leaders in some way, and that you do indeed have a purpose in which these skills are needed.

There is no such thing as coincidence or luck in this matter. If you want to find what you are here to do, or if you want to begin your path of serving, guiding, supporting, and healing others, the first thing you need to do is decide you are going to do it. The place to start is where you are — serving and helping everyone around you — and to know what that means.

If you want to connect with your spirit guide, for instance, all you need to do is decide you will and then ask the Universe to lead you to that experience. It will come to you, if that is where you put your will and intent and focus. The degree to which you are sure you want to connect with your guide will determine the speed with which you will be able to connect. You may feel led to read certain books, meet new people, and so forth, that will help show you the way.

How do you focus your will? One of the first ways is to remember a time in which you went after a goal and got it. As you think of that past experience, you bring that energy into your present reality. Remember a time in which you were intent on getting something and you got it. Say you wanted a new car. You went out and looked; you touched cars, drove them, thought about them, read about them, and attracted the money to buy one. Look at the level of dedication you put into achieving something, and you will see what is required to get something you want now.

Some of the things you wanted may have taken a long time to acquire. You can go back and realize that perhaps you did not have a high level of focus in obtaining them, or maybe you thought about them infrequently. Or you may have thought of them often but did not believe you could have them.

*The mind has 40,000 to 50,000
thoughts a day.
When you direct 1,000 to 2,000
of those daily thoughts to a goal,
it will come rapidly.*

Most of you think about something once, maybe two or three times a day, and then you wonder why it takes so long to get it. Thoughts are energy. The more you think about something, the more energy you bring from your inner world to create what you want to manifest in the outer world.

The number of thoughts you put into something and the intensity of emotional energy you have about something are important elements in determining how quickly you create it. Emotions propel thoughts into reality by their intensity. You need to maintain a consistent focus and desire and sustain them over a period of time to manifest what you want. The less doubt you have about getting something, the more rapidly it will come.

Think of a box that represents what you want. Every time you think about what you want, the box becomes fuller; and when critical mass is reached the box becomes reality. If there is something you think of repeatedly, at a certain point it will manifest. How long this takes is determined by both the strength of your belief that it will come and the intensity of your focus and desire to have it. This does not apply if what you want must come from other people, for you have control only over your reality, not theirs. Wanting something from people that they do not want to give will usually push them away.

The more you can believe you will have something, get excited, picture it in your mind, and feel the emotions of joy, excitement, and anticipation, the more quickly it will come. However, emotions of fear and doubt also create what they are focused on when you think of them over and over. When you fear something, you are thinking of what you do not want to happen, and it fills up a box labeled "What I do not want to happen." And sure enough, that box becomes full and then becomes reality.

If you want to focus your will more clearly, look at your doubts, the things in you that are saying, "I cannot have this." There are two boxes here — the box labeled "I can," which is filled with positive thoughts and joyful emotions, and the box labeled "I cannot," which is filled with fears and negative thoughts.

If you have many positive thoughts, but they are equally balanced by doubtful, fearful, or negative ones, you will create nothing. The desire for what you want must be stronger than your fears about not having it. Every time you fear something, you have less energy to create it. Do not make those fear thoughts wrong, but every time you recognize one, put positive thoughts alongside it.

After you are sure that you want to receive guidance, that you intend to do so and you feel positive and excited about it, you will then receive it. Reception of guidance takes place outside the mind and happens in a flash.

*If you look upward and focus on
higher realms, as surely as you breathe
you will receive any help or
information you need.*

The experience of the higher realms often comes in the form of inner seeing. All of you have had the experience of inner knowing, a 6th sense, a feeling that something was going to happen — and it did. You might have become aware, for instance, that someone you knew was going to receive something they had been wanting, and they did. Sometimes you look at people and you know something about them that you could not possibly know except by some added dimension of insight.

You have constant insights and revelations and new thoughts about your life. You receive telepathic messages instantaneously; there is usually no conscious awareness of their reception. I cannot tell you how to be aware of your telepathic reception of higher guidance, for it occurs outside of awareness. You first become aware of it through your thoughts and your inner seeing or sensing.

Suddenly you have a new way of handling a problem, or you experience a change in your consciousness. Either of these can be the first indication most of you have that you have received a broadcast. As this guidance and higher consciousness come into your emotional self, you soon find that old situations no longer trigger the same emotional response. As you bring the broadcast into your heart, you find yourself expanding and able to feel love and forgiveness where you did not before. You begin communicating ideas to others in new and different ways. As you receive higher ideas about your body, you may feel motivated to change your diet, exercise routine, or thoughts about your physical body.

The information is always there; one block is your lack of will and intent to receive the broadcast. Or you may be blocked because you are simply not paying attention. If you wish to receive more knowledge, love, and wisdom, all you need do is to focus upon having these and then take action when you receive the guidance to do so.

When you find yourself thinking mundane thoughts that go nowhere, taking time that you could spend in higher ways, think instead of the issues about which you want more information. Then be silent for a few moments and open to receive the broadcast. You will usually find some new bit of information or insight coming into your mind within an hour or so.

It is easy to receive from the Universal Mind; all you need to do is want to receive. The information may come to you through a friend or book; you may hear it or see it. It may come in the form of a new thought. You can open to it directly by getting into a relaxed state and quieting your mind. It is important to acknowledge when the guidance you seek has come. By connecting the thoughts, insights, and ideas you receive to your will and intent to obtain them, you strengthen your belief in your ability to receive intuitive guidance.

You are an independent individual who determines your own life and destiny by your will and intent. The more aware you are of the connection between what you want and its arrival in your physical reality, the more your ability to create what you want will increase. Whenever you have a new idea or a new thought and acknowledge it, you open yourself up to receiving more of them.

Writing down and recording your goals brings them to you faster.

What you want may be knowledge, an increased opportunity to serve, or the ability to be a channel of higher wisdom, for instance. You may want a business opportunity, a new career, or something else. Write down your intent and make it a clear message to the Universe: "I intend to write a book" or "I intend to discover my psychic and healing abilities, and I am now doing so." The clearer you can be about the direction you want to go in, the more quickly you can bring it about. You will begin to draw to yourself much information and guidance.

Another way is to affirm to yourself, when you are in a quiet space, that you would like new insights into your work. Be willing to recognize new insights, and then let go of the request. Monitor what comes into your thoughts during the day or even during the next half hour, just to experience what it feels like to receive from the higher levels.

Many have asked me, "How can I know the difference between my thoughts and the higher thoughts of the Universe?" For you wonder, "Was that a revelation, an inspiration, or was that my own mind thinking a wise thought?" There is no difference.

The telepathic reception of higher levels of knowledge is beyond your level of conscious awareness. You first become aware of it when it hits your thought processes. Some of you become aware of it sooner, such as when you are healing someone and you sense this person's energy. There are other ways of becoming aware of it, but the actual reception is beyond the scope of knowing. So you are asking, "How do I recognize it? How do I receive better?" If you want to receive better, if that is your desire, then you will. If you want to become more aware of your reception of guidance, then you will.

Every time you have a thought that seems to be outside of your normal range — for instance, you may be walking down the street and suddenly you come up with a new idea — you have received information from a higher realm. Many of you expect to hear a voice out of the sky telling you something; it is not usually that kind of experience. It usually feels like your own mind or imagination.

By the time you are aware of reception, the information is already in your world of form, which is your thoughts. The ideas feel like your own thoughts, but they have a higher quality to them. They are of a different nature; they bring a new way of looking at something or a more loving perspective.

A new, original thought can be a sign that you are in tune with that higher level of guidance. The more you validate it, the more you acknowledge that you have picked up telepathic messages, the more often you will get them. You will find that it becomes increasingly boring to think at your old levels; you get tired of running the same problems around in your mind when it can be so rewarding to receive inspiration and insights. Boredom is often a tool of the soul to lure you into new spaces.

*If you want
to bring in guidance,
start by sitting quietly.*

There are many altered states of consciousness that you experience in the normal course of the day. When you get lost in a book or the internet, when you watch TV, when you drift off to the sounds of beautiful music, when you daydream, paint, or play a musical instrument, you are in a state of altered consciousness. These states are associated with the right brain, your creative nature, and are the states that most influence your ability to receive higher guidance. You receive guidance through the right, or creative, side of your brain; it is then translated through the left-brain side of memory and logic into concrete information. Whenever you become quiet, you are in a more receptive state.

Your challenge at these times is to tune out mundane and idle thoughts and focus your attention upward. When you think of other people in this quiet state of receptivity, you can receive their emotional or mental energy. It may lower your own energy to think of them if they are depressed or in pain.

When you receive telepathically from the higher levels of the Universe, you move up into your higher self. As you become more loving and full of light, you can bring up the energy of others also. They may not go as high as you (and some may go higher), but you can raise the vibration of everyone around you by tuning your awareness higher.

As you sit quietly, ask for guidance. Then, be willing to listen. Notice your body. Perhaps you will feel a physical sensation like a tingling as you focus upward. Ask for guidance, stating clearly your question. Keep random thoughts from pulling on your attention. If you can focus for even five minutes on what you want guidance on, you will receive a new way of thinking and a higher outlook in that short length of time. Your call is always heard; the only problem comes in your ability to listen.

How do you broadcast healing to others? You touch people; you speak to them; you write and send out your knowledge.

When it is your intent to connect with others from your higher centers, your words, writings, and touch come from that place.

You may say, "How do I know if I am saying the right words, touching the body in just the right way for healing?" If the intent is to be healing, then the words and the touch will always be right for that person. There is no error at this level. Only your mind and personality can create judgment and error.

Whenever you have the intent to heal, no matter what process you use, what form or technique you try, you will be healing. The other person must also want the healing, for if they are not ready then nothing you try will work. Remember, too, that you are not healing other people; you are creating the space as you work with them for them to heal themselves.

If you are feeling angry and want to get back at someone, then your intent is clearly not healing. If you try to speak nice words to cover your anger, you are not healing. There is no lying at this level. If you go about your day with the intent to heal and lift the energy around you, then everywhere you go — to the grocery store, office, or down the street — you will be a healing, lifting influence, even though you may not be consciously offering this energy.

> *It is up to you
> to create the specific form
> your work will take.*

The guidance that is available to you is unlimited in whatever form you choose and whatever field you choose, be it business, the healing arts, performing arts, science, education, or something else. The will to do anything draws you to the information and guidance you need in that area.

The main function of the higher centers of telepathy is to attune you with your higher purpose, help you discover what you came here to do, and bring to you the information and opportunities you need to do it. As you experience working in these higher levels, you will increase your ability to be a loving influence on those around you and increase your ability to see with your inner eyes. The intent to do so is all that is necessary to attune yourself to the higher realms of guidance.

Playsheet

Chapter 16

Receiving Guidance from the Higher Realms

1. Think of five specific things that you asked for and received guidance on last year, such as a decision, problem, or a choice you needed to make.
2. Think of something in your life you want guidance on right now. Sit quietly, ask for guidance, and notice if any new thoughts come to you. Record or note these.

SECTION II

Clearing Energy

CHAPTER 17

Orin's Introduction to Clearing Energy

Orin: As you have read and worked with the processes in this book, you have learned many ways to become aware of your energy and other people's energy. You have developed skill in listening to your intuition and paying attention to telepathic messages. You have discovered how to be aware of the unseen energies about you, noticing when you have taken on or been affected by them. Throughout this, you have been learning how to be true to yourself. With this awareness, you now have a greater ability to be the creator of your life and to gain the personal power that this awareness brings.

Over the years since this book was first published, many readers have let us know of their challenges in remaining clear and unaffected by the energies they are around. They asked for more help and guidance to do so. In response, I offer additional information, processes, and guidance you can use to further evolve your energy skills. You can use these to strengthen your ability to recognize and release unwanted energy through a process that I call "clearing energy."

I invite you to explore these additional skills and techniques that, when practiced, will increase your ability to sustain freer, clearer, higher states no matter what energies you are around.

As you continue, you will explore how to clear energy by connecting with your innermost divine Self to dissolve thoughts and emotions that may take you out of your calm, clear center. You will learn more about the nature of the energy you are clearing, how not to be affected by it, and how to let it go.

As you stay in a clear, higher space, you can more continually experience the well-being that is your natural state of consciousness. I invite you to take your next steps of gaining personal power through clearing energy.

Clearing Energy with Your Divine Self

W hen you are free of lesser energies, you feel more joyful, insightful, focused, and optimistic. You are your true Self, the Self you are when you are not affected by the energies around. In a clear state you are more open to life and love. You feel alive! You are in the flow, motivated, productive, and creative.

What does it feel like
to be clear?
It feels wonderful!

When you are clear you have the enthusiasm and energy you need to accomplish your goals. Regrets, fears, and doubts recede, and confidence and clarity take their place. You are open and receptive to your higher good. You embrace change and new things. What seemed like problems or obstructions disappear, and burdens fall away. You feel good about yourself, your life, and other people.

Being in a clear state allows you to open to new possibilities and unfold the greater potential of your life. Being clear makes it easier to recognize that which is your purpose and that which is not. You strengthen your ability to bring about your higher good, working in harmony with the Universe.

As you clear energy that may be affecting you, and you open to higher energies, the channel expands between you and your innermost divine Self. You can experience a greater downflow of spiritual energy and guidance. Taking action on this guidance brings your inner divine light into outer manifestation as forms, relationships, experiences, and circumstances. What you create will fulfill its purpose and bring you even more than you could think to ask for. When you are clear, you can experience more of the love that is who you truly are. With your increasing radiance you become a beacon of light to an ever-widening circle of people.

You have already experienced being clear during those times when you felt good about yourself and your life.

Reflect on times in the past when you experienced being clear, in touch with your innermost Self and your truth. Among other feelings, you may have felt confident and good about yourself, inspired, happy, and in charge of your life. Some other indications that you were in a clear space are a sense of well-being, loving and supportive thoughts of yourself and others, and feeling balanced and at peace with the world. Recall these feelings and allow yourself to feel this way right now.

You can feel this way whenever you choose by recognizing when you do not feel this way and then taking steps to return to loving, harmonious states where you are clear and can experience the light of the divine shining through you.

For the next several days, notice when you feel balanced and in your center. Acknowledge that you are clear during those times. Become familiar with how you experience being in a clear state mentally, emotionally, and physically. If you feel like you have taken on unwanted energy, use the process and information that follows, as well as anything else you have learned, to return to a balanced, peaceful state.

> *One of the greatest challenges to being clear is recognizing when you are not clear.*

Throughout this book, you have been learning about how to recognize the subtle energies that are all around you. You have become more aware of the energies you are exposed to throughout the day, including those that do not reflect the reality you want to experience. These can be beliefs, concepts, thoughts, emotions, fears, worries, and cultural conditioning that exist in the environment. They can come from other people or simply appear in your consciousness. You may have experienced them so often that they have become your normal way of thinking and being, and you may not even be aware that things could be different or that these are not your thoughts.

You can know in part that you need to clear your energy by the way you feel. Some indications you are not clear are:

feeling stressed, anxious, angry, discouraged, powerless, or worried. You may have a strong emotional response to something that surprises you and is unusual for you. These feelings are not who you are! They come from energy you live around that you have picked up and thought was your own.

Other ways you can know you have picked up energy that is not yours: when you experience thoughts that bring you down and make you feel vulnerable or scared, have thoughts that circle around without resolution, or picture negative outcomes. Other ways you can know you are not clear is when you have trouble concentrating, feel unbalanced, are worried about a future event, or experience deep concern about your life or relationships. You may feel others do not love you. You may experience regret or guilt or self-recrimination or find yourself dwelling on past mistakes. You may have worried thoughts about money and paying your bills, or about your job, relationships, or health. Anytime you do not have a sense of well-being, assume you have taken on energy that does not reflect your true Self.

You can rise above mass consciousness and experience divine consciousness instead.

You live in a sea of energies I call "mass consciousness." It is composed of thoughts, beliefs, concepts, opinions, judgments, emotions, fears, and energy built up over the ages by lesser-evolved members of humanity. People have passed down their beliefs, thoughts, and cultural conditioning from generation to generation. Babies are born into this swirl of thoughts and beliefs and quickly pick them up. You may have unknowingly accepted certain mass beliefs as your own that do not reflect your truth.

*It is not difficult to clear energy.
You can do so by contacting your divine Self.*

In this book I have referred to your higher self and soul as sources of light and guidance that are within you, which you can work with to become more aware of the subtle energies around you. Since you have been contacting your higher self and soul, your inner light has increased, and you have greatly evolved your consciousness. You are now ready to connect with an even higher aspect of your being that I call your "divine Self." This Self with a capital *S* is within you and includes the consciousness of your soul and higher self. It is also known as Spirit, the Presence, the One Life.

Opening to the light of your higher self and soul allows you to become aware of the greater light of your divine Self. This Self is the source of light and life within you. Working with the unseen energies from this level of light expands your ability to recognize and release unwanted energy.

Do not worry about being able to tell the difference between the various levels of your being, such as between your higher self, soul, and divine Self. Simply have the intention to connect with your divine Self and you will. This Self is aware that you want to connect with It and is assisting you in doing so.

Staying clear does not come from using willpower or trying to force yourself to let go of thoughts, feelings, and other energies that you do not want. It starts with recognizing that you are not clear. You do not have to fight these energies or deny them to release them. Being clear comes from contacting your highest, innermost Self, which then works with you to clear the way. As you work with this Self, It dissolves thoughts and feelings that are holding you back.

*Lower energies can have no power
over you. They are not supported
by any spiritual law or truth.*

Many times you give power to unwanted thoughts, feelings, beliefs, stories, and memories. You may feel that they are simply showing you reality the way it is. Or you may have tried to release them without success. You do not need to let regrets, guilt, memories, or negative beliefs hold you back. You do not need to fear that future events will harm you or stop you. You do not need to live with worry or a lack of self-confidence.

As you connect with your divine Self, you know that these lesser, unwanted thoughts, beliefs, and feelings can have no real power over you and cannot control you. When you open to your divine Self and allow Its light to shine on them, they disappear, because they are not backed by any spiritual laws or truth.

Your innermost divine Self, the One Life within you, is all powerful. This means that there is *no other* power. Even though these lesser energies feel real when viewed from the personality level, when viewed with the illumination of the divine Self they can be seen to have no true power. There is nothing to fight against, for they have no substance and are not real.

When you encounter these kinds of energies, start by affirming something such as "These negative feelings and thoughts exist 'out there' and are not mine. They can have no power over me because they are not supported by any spiritual law or truth. Even though they feel very real, they are appearing in my mind because I have picked them up from the mass consciousness that is all around me."

*Unwanted, lesser energies disappear
in the light of your divine Self.*

As you connect with your innermost Self, you can experience Its divine consciousness of abundance and love, harmony and well-being. With this contact you realize that these mass-consciousness thoughts and beliefs need not control or affect you.

The energies that come from mass consciousness are like a mirage that evaporates when you get closer to it. You realize nothing was ever there except in your mind. It is the same with the energies you want to clear. All you need to do is connect with your divine Self and experience Its light and consciousness that knows the true, unreal nature of these energies. When you do this they begin to disappear. Any power you have given them diminishes, until they are no longer a problem. Eventually they do not even enter into your awareness.

Events in ordinary reality change when you work from this level of light and truth. Unwanted thoughts, feelings, memories, and fears have less effect on you. If they do arise, they are not as strong and you recognize them more easily. You no longer fall into the temptation to believe that there is anything that can have power over you. You stop listening to your own or other people's stories that create fear or worry. Blockages disappear and the future opens up in wonderful and unexpected ways.

*To clear unwanted thoughts, emotions,
memories, and beliefs, impersonalize them.
Do not identify with them as yours.*

Another principle in effectively clearing energy is to recognize that all energy is simply impersonal energy that exists "out there" in mass consciousness. There is a tendency to make the energy you have taken on personal, as if it truly is who you are. For instance, if you pick up scattered, off-balance, upset, or fearful energy, you might be tempted to think, "I feel scattered, off-balance, upset, fearful," and so on. You have made these energies personal and accepted them as yours. These are simply energies that you have picked up from mass consciousness, and they are *not* your energy.

Realize that you have picked up thoughts, beliefs, and feelings from your environment that are covering up your ability to act and think in higher ways. You simply have not known what to do to effectively shift and release them. You identified with them and let them define you, but now you can recognize that they are not you and release them.

You can clear energy more easily than you think.

Impersonalizing the energy in this way is an important step to take, for when you stop accepting or identifying with these thoughts, beliefs, or feelings, you can release them — and you can do so more easily than you think. Notice how much more powerful you feel each time you impersonalize energy that has been affecting you.

Do not assign these impersonal energies to another person. Even though it may seem as if people are expressing fear, lack, and limitation, recognize that they, too, took on energy that they need to clear. They are not the source of these energies. Other people simply act as a "delivery vehicle" to bring these impersonal energies to you for you to clear. If it is not one person, it will be another, until you learn to "nothingize" these energies, impersonalize them, and shine the illumination of your divine Self upon them. Recognize that all of these are impersonal energies that exist around you in the environment, no matter who seems to be caught up in them, yourself included.

With the understanding that these energies are not personal, you have increasing compassion for yourself and others, knowing that other people are just as much a victim of these energies as you have been.

> *You can choose what energies,*
> *thoughts, and influences*
> *to allow into your consciousness.*

You can learn to become aware of the energy you are around and notice anytime lesser energies are affecting you. Staying clear requires ongoing attention, lasting a lifetime. Measure your progress not by your success in never taking on negative energy, but by how quickly you recognize you have done so and by your growing ability to return to a wonderful, clear, flowing state.

Do not expect to be clear all the time, or even to immediately recognize when you have accepted energy that you will later need to release. This takes practice, observation, and the increasing spiritual illumination that comes through contact with your divine Self.

As you continue to clear, you get faster at recognizing when you have been affected by unwanted thoughts and emotions. You expect to feel good! You no longer spend days or hours feeling low or discouraged. You recognize that this is not your normal state and that you have picked up energy you need to clear. You then connect with your divine Self to know this unwanted energy for the nothingness that it is, returning to a balanced, clear state as it disappears.

Once you get clear in one area, you may become aware that there are other areas you need to shift through releasing unwanted energy. Do not think that you are going backward just because more issues have come up for you to clear once you set your intention to stay in a clear state. At first it may seem as if there are energies to release and clear everywhere you look.

Clearing work is cumulative.
You are peeling off layer after layer.

The more you clear energy, such as doubts and fears, for example, the less you are tempted to take on this kind of energy and the more often you experience confidence and courage in its place.

Releasing and clearing energy is not just a mental exercise. It happens through increasing your inner light and working with your true, innermost divine Self. To get results, you will need to make a real connection to your divine Self and not just read about doing so. Use the playsheet that follows to learn how to connect with your divine Self and how to clear any energy you encounter.

What you consider to be a high, clear state today may be just a taste of how good you will feel as you continue connecting with your true, innermost Self and clear any energy that veils your inner light and truth. As your illumination increases, limiting thoughts and beliefs begin to dissolve, disappear, and no longer affect you, even if you are around them. When your energy is clear, you are magnetic to ideas, opportunities, inspiration, abundance, and people. Disharmony turns into harmony, turmoil into peace, self-doubt into self-confidence, and self-pity into self-esteem.

*Your clear energy is a gift
to everyone around you.*

As you keep your energy clear and sustain a higher state of consciousness, you offer clear energy to everyone around you. You become a source of light and stability to an ever-widening circle of people and to all life.

PLAYSHEET

Chapter 18

Clearing Energy with Your Divine Self

This is a summary of the steps involved in clearing energy. Use this as a guide for the exercises on clearing that follow. The process of clearing does not need to take long. Once you learn these steps, you can apply them in a few short moments. The most important step is to make contact with your divine Self to increase your inner light.

1. **Set your intention** to recognize and clear any energy that is keeping you from experiencing the radiance, joy, love, and harmony that is your true nature.
2. **Think of something to clear.** Let a thought, memory, belief, or feeling come to mind that you would like to clear, something that is causing you stress or an out-of-balance feeling.
3. **Connect with your divine Self.** In a moment of inner peace and stillness, connect with your divine Self. You can do this in a few seconds, although taking longer is good as well. You might say, "I am open, I am receptive, I am asking for help to clear (whatever you want)." Pause for a moment in stillness and wait. Even 10 to 20 seconds is all you need to make contact and receive a response.

   Note that contact happens in a moment beyond words and thoughts, so you may have no awareness of making contact or receiving a response. Your intention to connect with your divine Self and your receptivity to It are all that is needed to make this connection and receive energy back. Know that your divine Self is aware of your desire to connect and always responds.

4. **Sense your inner light.** Imagine this connection to your divine Self filling you with light. You might picture this light as a pillar, column, or channel of light that runs through the middle of your body, around your spine. It rises straight up to your divine Self. This inner light shines out from you like a light bulb shines out. Your inner light shines brightly.

5. **Realize these energies can have no power over you.** As you shine your inner light upon whatever you want to clear, recognize that this energy has no power because it is not supported by any spiritual law or truth. You do not need to fight it or work hard to push it away.

6. **Impersonalize these energies; do not identify with them.** Affirm that these unwanted thoughts and feelings are *not* you. They are energies you have picked up from mass consciousness. In order to release these, it is important not to identify with them but to simply view them as impersonal energies that exist "out there."

7. **Turn them into nothing.** The light of your divine Self shining through you reveals the nothingness of all lesser, lower energies. There is no need to get rid of them, because they never existed. They are like the mirage in the desert that only seems real until you approach it. They are inconsequential, temporary, transitory energies that are easy to dissipate. Watch them fade into nothingness in the light you are holding upon them.

Evaluation

Notice whether anything has shifted, even in a small or subtle way, in how you feel or think about that area or situation.

Perhaps you feel less worried or concerned, or it feels like some burden has been lifted. You may have a better feeling or feel physically more relaxed as you think of it. You may not be as drawn to think about that particular issue anymore, and other issues now seem more important. And you may forget about your concerns altogether.

Because you live in a world of time, the story you have about an area — your thoughts and feelings about it — will often shift over time, and you may not immediately experience the full results of your clearing work. However, the clearing you have done is real, and the work is cumulative. Every time you clear energy, you reduce the number of things you need to clear in the future.

You do not have to spend a lot of time clearing; in fact, it is very effective to have frequent 10- or 20-second periods of divine Self contact throughout the day, or whenever you notice you have taken on energy that you want to release. Do this even if it is a single thought or worry; take the time to clear it so it does not attract more of the same.

CHAPTER 19

Clearing Suggestions

What follows are suggestions of energies you can clear, using the clearing process discussed in the playsheet that precedes this chapter. In the following clearing suggestions I do not repeat all these steps, since you can refer to and use the clearing process in addition to the suggestions below. Pick those you feel drawn to, and enjoy!

Clearing Thoughts

It is important to recognize and clear thoughts you do not want, particularly those that are stressful and that do not benefit or empower you. You may have experienced feeling good, then a thought crossed your mind that immediately changed your mood. It may have been a thought that caused you to feel anxiety, worry, or fear. Perhaps you were enjoying working on something until you started having thoughts that you might not succeed or that other people might not approve. The list of discouraging thoughts is endless. Each thought can attract more thoughts of a similar nature and start you on a downward spiral, chipping away at your self-esteem.

It can change your life to become aware of and let go of unwanted thoughts that undermine you. Be alert to any random, stray thoughts that take away your confidence and enthusiasm. Watch for stressful thoughts, such as those that cause you to doubt yourself.

If these kinds of thoughts come up, do not engage with them, fight them, or think they are true. Recognize that these are not yours but thoughts that you have picked up from the general environment that you need to clear.

Make contact with your divine Self and shine Its light on any unwanted thoughts until they fade from your awareness. You do not need to pay attention to them or give them any validity. They are not based on or supported by any spiritual laws or truth. As you stop identifying with them, they lose their ability to affect you. They disappear in the spiritual light that radiates from the core of your being.

Doing this frees you from any limitations these unwanted thoughts place on you. When you are clear, your thoughts will be supportive and encouraging. Enjoy all the insightful, inspiring, and positive thoughts you can have when you connect with your divine Self!

One woman found that contacting her divine Self and using the clearing energy process made a big difference in her ability to move forward with a project she was working on. She believed the project was a worthy one that would make a contribution to people's lives. The Universe seemed to support her efforts, and things were going well. Then, for what seemed like no reason, she started feeling overwhelmed by thoughts of failure and other limiting thoughts. These almost stopped her from moving ahead. After she learned about clearing unwanted thoughts, she decided to face them and no longer accept them as true.

She started shining the light of her divine Self on the thoughts as they arose. She was happy to find that these kinds of thoughts began to lessen in their intensity, many never to return.

With practice she now quickly identifies limiting thoughts and does not let them affect her. She realizes she has picked them up from the pool of "thoughts" that exist out in the world and that they are not her thoughts. Now she shines her inner light upon them, allowing them to fade out and disappear.

Sometimes they leave right away, and other times she needs to shine her inner light on them several times to stop them from coming into her mind. As she does this, she experiences an inflow of positive, insightful thoughts that give her confidence to move forward.

Several people have let us know that the process of clearing energy was very helpful when a friend or loved one suddenly stopped returning their calls, stopped speaking to them, or ghosted them on social media.

One woman, for example, spent weeks trying to figure out what she had said or done, and still could not fathom why her friend had suddenly pulled away and stopped responding to her. She had thoughts that she was unlovable, that she was not acceptable, and many other thoughts that made her doubt herself and feel afraid to create new friendships.

By connecting with her divine Self she was able to shine her spiritual light on self-depreciating thoughts whenever they arose. This helped her avoid being drawn into feelings of despair, anger, or defensiveness. She practiced not accepting these undermining thoughts as her reality, knowing that they were not real, had no power, and were not supported by any spiritual law or truth.

She began to recognize that these self-critical thoughts were not showing her the truth — that she was a good, loving person and that there was nothing wrong with her.

When any thoughts arose that made her doubt that she was lovable, she connected with her divine Self and radiated light to those thoughts. She soon found that negative self-images were replaced by positive ones as she trusted and believed in herself. She said she realized afterward that the relationship had not been good for her, and that it turned out to be a blessing that the relationship no longer existed. She also reported finding new friends who were much more compatible and supportive.

Clearing Emotions

You have probably experienced feeling calm one moment, then feeling irritated, anxious, sad, or upset the next, without any apparent cause. Or you might have been around someone who is experiencing these emotions and suddenly felt the same way yourself.

Emotions can be contagious. When everyone is feeling happy, you may find yourself feeling happy. However, when people around you are feeling strong, unhappy emotions, you may also find yourself feeling those emotions as if they were yours. People do not even need to be physically present for you to pick up their emotions.

If you experience strong emotions that take you out of your center, no matter what the apparent cause, start by affirming that these are *not* yours even if they seem to arise from within you. You do not need to fight them or suppress them. Connect with your innermost divine Self in a moment of inner stillness. Feel the light of your divine Self radiating from the center of your being, calming your emotions, until their intensity decreases and you feel more peaceful.

Pay attention to your emotions today. If you experience upsetting ones, recognize that you are responding to emotions that are floating around in the general field of energy you live in. The emotions that are "out there" may trigger similar ones in yourself; however, you do not need to feel them or identify with them as yours.

If the emotions you are experiencing are very strong, you may need to repeatedly connect with your divine Self and experience Its inner light until you can maintain a sense of peace. You may also want to shine light on any negative thoughts generated by these emotions. Afterward, enjoy being in a peaceful inner state.

Clearing Negative Memories

Many people feel burdened by past memories that can bring up feelings of regret, guilt, humiliation, hurt, or self-recrimination. These memories can drain your energy and take the joy out of living.

If you have some memory or past event that you play over and over in your mind, or something you wish you could have done differently, you can release the pain and suffering you have caused yourself by repeatedly recalling it.

Start by forgiving yourself. You did the best you knew how at the level of consciousness you were at during that time of your life. You were acting on misperceptions, limiting beliefs, and negative thoughts you picked up from your family and friends, from the culture you grew up in, and from the general "thought" environment that was around you.

You can become aware of unpleasant memories and stop being affected by them. These might be memories that make you feel bad about yourself. Perhaps you have a memory of feeling unloved or unappreciated, or you recall times that others hurt you. Maybe you regret something you did and wish you could do it over. You may be going over and over a conversation, wishing you had provided a better answer or said something different. You might remember something you failed at, and this memory is keeping you from trying again. If this happens, take a moment to recall the memory, the story you are telling yourself, and the people involved.

Connect with your innermost Self and ask It to clear the thoughts and emotions that are connected to this memory. It is time to stop hurting yourself by continually remembering something you feel bad about. Allow your divine Self to flood your consciousness with forgiveness. Shine Its light upon this memory and let it fade away. It is just a memory and it has no power. You have learned all you need from it, and in some way this event made you stronger and wiser.

Afterward, if this memory returns, notice how it is different. Perhaps it has less effect on you, or you have gained new insights and understanding about it. You may find so little energy around this memory that you completely let it go. Let yourself feel the joy that comes when you leave the past in the past and experience your true, confident Self.

Clearing Obstructions, Blockages, and Stuck Places

If you would like to open up an area where you feel blocked or stuck, think of it now. If it is a very large area affecting many aspects of your life and has been a problem for a long time, let come to mind some smaller part of this challenge on which you can focus your light.

Connect with your divine Self and feel Its light shining out from the center of your being. As you think of this area, ask to become aware of any thoughts, beliefs, emotions, or memories that are holding you back. You might catch thoughts arising that tell you that the situation is difficult or hopeless, that there is nothing you can do, that you have tried everything, that others who are involved will not cooperate, and so on.

Shine the clear light of your divine Self onto any self-depreciating thoughts, feelings, and memories that come up. Let them fade away into nothingness. Affirm that any thoughts telling you that you are limited or stuck are not real and do not have any power over you. Determine that you are not going to pay attention to them or give them any validity. Lack and limitation are not supported by any spiritual laws or truth.

As you do this, you open up the energy around this situation, and things will change. Results start on the inner, so be alert to any changes in your feelings, thoughts, or story about the situation. Perhaps you feel lighter, as if a burden has been lifted. Keep repeating this process as more thoughts and realizations come to the surface. Shifts in your feelings and thoughts will eventually appear as shifts in the outer world, such as new opportunities and positive changes in your existing circumstances.

As you continue to connect with your innermost Self and shine Its light on this situation, you will discover that this Self has gone ahead of you and cleared the path, opening a way for you to move forward in this area. Be willing to have your life work and to accept that you can create a fulfilling life more easily than you imagined.

Clearing Your Pets

Pets, and in fact all animals, are just as vulnerable as you are to taking on energy. They are very sensitive and pick up people's thoughts and emotions. They live out the beliefs and pictures people send them about their health, bodies, behavior, emotional states, and relationships to humans and other animals.

Let one worrisome or negative thought you have had about a pet — yours or someone else's — come to mind so you can clear it. Shine the light of your divine Self onto this thought until it begins to fade. You can dispel this thought easily, so that it can no longer affect this pet.

Let come to mind thoughts and pictures you are holding about this pet's aging. Are you picturing health or disability? Include thoughts you have about the pet's mobility, dental health, eyes, and mental condition, for now and in the future. Are there any thoughts or pictures you would like to let go of? If so, clear them as they arise.

Think of this pet right now without any negative thoughts or pictures about its past or an imagined future. Shine the light of your divine Self on this pet to help unfold the divine plan for it. Listen to and follow whatever inner urges you have about what to provide for this pet in the way of experiences, living conditions, food, time with you and others, love, and good care. Be open to any inner guidance about this pet and what it needs from you.

If other thoughts, pictures, memories, emotions, or worries about your or others' pets come to mind, shine the light of your divine Self on them. Catch yourself before you project a negative thought onto a pet. Instead, shine your inner light on this pet. As you radiate the light of the divine, you are helping this pet evolve and fulfill more of its potential.

Clearing an Object

Some of the objects in your home, office, or other environments may carry energy from the past, from others who have
owned or used them, energies of the person who has given
them to you, or any other energy that might not be as high
and light-filled as you would like.

In your mind's eye, scan your home or environment and
sense if there are any objects that seem to draw your attention
because they feel darker or simply do not feel as if they belong
there. Trust that whatever objects come to mind to clear are
perfect, and that for some reason you need to fill these objects
with light or remove them to help lift the vibration of your
environment. Once you have discovered an object to clear, use
the instructions for clearing a space, a home, and the general
environment that follow.

Clearing a Space, a Home,
and the General Environment

Think of an object or a place you want to clear, such as your
home, office, or any other environment. Connect with your
divine Self in silence until you feel more peaceful and aware.
Feel your central column of light shining out from you. Shine
this inner light on each room and on all the objects within it.
In your mind's eye, and using your imagination, notice if you
sense any place that seems darker or deader in some way, or that
has less flowing energy. There may be leftover energy from an
angry or unhappy person who spent time in that room. Trust
whatever you sense, feel, or imagine as you scan each area.

Radiate light to clear this place or the objects within it.
Or simply observe as the energy in these places comes into

harmony with the light you are radiating. Notice that dishar-
monious energies disappear as you shine light upon them.
The area, objects, and room begin to feel more light-filled
and open. Afterward, listen to any guidance you might receive
about rearranging your furniture and objects, selling or giving
things away, putting things into storage, or moving things
around so that your environment can reflect this greater light.

Keep repeating this process until you can put your awareness into all areas of your environment and the objects in it,
feeling that these areas are clear and that they support you in
feeling good. This may be an ongoing process, for energy is
dynamic and ever-changing.

One couple took a vacation and let a down-and-out friend
stay in their home for several weeks while they were gone.
Their friend had had very little energy and had slept most of
the time, feeling depressed and out of sorts. When the couple
got home, the woman who had made her home available
to the friend started feeling tired and drained, even though
this was not her normal state. Because her spouse felt normal
(energy does not affect everyone the same way), she did not
think about the possibility that she had picked up energy from
their friend. Instead, for several weeks she kept thinking of
reasons why she felt so tired and unbalanced, and she tried
every remedy that came to mind.

One day she remembered what she knew about clearing
energy and decided to see if the tiredness she was feeling
came from her friend's energy that was still in the house.
Sure enough, as she connected with her divine Self and radiated this light throughout her home, she could feel a shift in
herself. Within an hour she felt like her usual self, energetic
and clearheaded.

In another case, a man at the peak of his career moved into a home that had previously been owned by a couple who had to sell the home for financial reasons. Once he moved in, he would wake up in the middle of the night with thoughts such as "You are a failure, your career is going nowhere," followed by feelings of deep discouragement. He kept reasoning with himself that he was doing fine and that there was nothing to worry about, but the troubling thoughts and feelings kept appearing.

Even though he had studied how to clear negative energy, it took him several months of battling these thoughts and feelings before he remembered that these thoughts were not his. He then worked with them as impersonal energies that had no power over him.

Since most of these thoughts occurred in the bedroom, he radiated the light of his divine Self throughout that room. This was where the previous owner had slept and where these thoughts were still lingering. He also took each thought and feeling as it arose into the light of his divine Self. Soon after, thoughts and feelings of this kind had disappeared and he was back to his normal, confident self.

Clearing for Success and Best Outcome

Think of some activity, project, event, decision, meeting, or whatever comes to mind for which you would like to experience the highest possible outcome.

What negative thoughts, concerns, fears, or worrisome pictures about this area and the outcome can you become aware of? Perhaps you have a list of possible problems you think may happen, or perhaps you doubt your abilities or vision. You may be concerned that someone might stand in the way or otherwise try to block your efforts. You might be afraid to hope for the best outcome because you do not want to be disappointed.

As you become aware of disquieting thoughts that would keep you from creating the highest outcome, affirm that these thoughts are not yours, that they do not come from your divine Self, and that you are not going to identify with them. They are energies that exist "out there" that you have picked up. They have no substance and are not real.

Contact your divine Self and sense your inner light shining out from the core of your being. Bring into the light each thought, picture, fear, or concern that might block your efforts. Each time you clear these unreal, powerless energies, they will have less effect on you, until they no longer come into your awareness.

Open to any guidance, insights, and uplifting thoughts that you can now access. Enjoy thinking of all the positive outcomes you can now experience!

Clearing before Being with People

Think of a person or group of people you will be connecting with today or sometime in the near future. To create a positive outcome, you can clear energy before you interact with people.

Reflect on times you have connected with this person or group in the past. Are there memories from the past that would interfere with experiencing a great connection right now? Are there any judgments, worries, or concerns that you are holding in your mind that you may or may not be aware of? Is there anything you can think of that could affect your ability to create a good outcome?

Contact your divine Self in a moment of silence. Shine your inner light on whatever thoughts, emotions, or memories come into your awareness that you do not want affecting your upcoming interactions. Affirm that these do not reflect truth and that you are ready to let them go.

Work with those that come up. Do not worry if you cannot discover all of the thoughts and memories that could affect your upcoming time together. You need to clear only those that come into your awareness. Each time you do this, new or different thoughts may appear for you to clear, depending on the people who will be joining you and the circumstances of your time together.

As you shine light on these old memories and thoughts, affirm that they are not telling you the truth, they are not from the light, and they can have no power over you. Watch them fade and disappear, knowing they will no longer shape your interactions with this person or group of people.

Ask your divine Self to infuse you with wisdom, love, and understanding. You are connecting with this person or these people with openness and positive energy. You are receptive to whatever needs to come about to unfold the higher purpose of your time together.

Listen to your inner guidance and let it reveal anything about this upcoming group meeting or interaction that you need to pay attention to so you can create the best outcome. Focus on the opportunities that exist for this connection and the good that you can create together.

One woman who was a manager for her company reported that she experienced a big shift using the clearing process before an upcoming meeting with both staff and higher-ups. In the past the meetings had often run overtime and were somewhat contentious. Even though she was the manager, she continued to encounter resistance to new programs she was responsible for implementing.

She wanted the big company meeting to go well, since she was presenting a number of new programs that she hoped would be met with interest rather than people's usual resistance to change.

Before the meeting, she determined to clear every negative thought and picture she was holding, such as thoughts that people would take a lot of convincing and that she would have to spend much time and energy dealing with resistance. She opened to the light of her divine Self and took into Its light each negative thought that came up, recognizing that they had no power over her or what would happen.

She went into the meeting free from her past memories and negative thoughts. She was open to having divine perfection unfold in the meeting. Afterward, she was almost in disbelief about how well the meeting went. The energy of the meeting was flowing, cooperative, and productive. People were receptive and responded to her suggested changes with interest and support. She was so amazed at the results that she vowed to release any preconceived ideas and negative expectations before every future meeting.

Clearing after Being with People

You can clear any energy you have taken on from others after interacting with them. It is helpful to sense your energy before you connect with people so that you can detect if and how you feel different afterward.

After you connect with a person or group of people, review how you feel. Do you feel tired, whereas before you connected with them you felt good? Do you feel bad about life or yourself in any way, whereas before contact you felt uplifted and positive? Did they make statements about reality that you do not want as your truth? Do you feel less focused and more scattered, whereas before you interacted you were able to concentrate on your priorities? Are you feeling doubt, anxiety, concern, or worry that was not there before you interacted with this person or people? Are you having trouble focusing on your own life because you are still thinking about the life and problems of that person or group? All of these are signs that you need to connect with your divine Self and clear any energy you brought into yourself that is not yours.

Call upon your divine Self in a moment of silence. Allow Its radiant light to shine onto every thought, feeling, or disturbance that comes up.

Lower energies vanish when looked at in the light of truth that you are now shining upon them. This light reveals that these energies are not real. They are easy to release. One by one, let any unwanted energies fade away until they no longer come into your awareness. You can then return to your natural, clear, peaceful state.

Do not blame other people either, for they are not the source of these energies. They, too, have taken on energy they do not know how to clear. These unwanted thoughts are simply impersonal energies that come from "out there," even if it seems that other people passed them on to you.

These lesser energies are not who you are! Your true, clear self is a confident, radiant being. Each time you clear energy, the effects of that type of energy become weaker and weaker, until you no longer respond to it or it no longer comes into your mind.

Clearing at the End of the Day

Reviewing your day before you go to sleep can be a wonderful way to discover and clear any energy you have picked up that is not yours and does not represent the truth of your being. This helps you sleep more soundly and wake up with more energy.

Before falling asleep, make contact with your divine Self during a few moments of inner stillness. Open to receive all that It has for you in the moment. Every contact, whether you are aware of your divine Self or not, strengthens your ability to create a fulfilling life.

Sit quietly after you connect with your divine Self and listen within. Ask your innermost Self to bring to your awareness any energy you need to clear from the day. As you do this, you might become aware of whether you have picked up any beliefs about reality or negative pictures about the future that you do not want as yours, perhaps from being around others, through the news, or from other sources. You might have picked up negative beliefs about aging, your body, relationships, or abundance, or other thoughts you want to release.

Scan your emotions. Are you experiencing any of the emotional energy you were around, such as irritation, discouragement, upset, or other unsettling feelings? Think of anytime you felt slightly off-balance, less confident, or unsure of yourself. Identify the thoughts and beliefs that might have triggered these feelings, or the general energy that led to them. If they are still with you, link with your divine Self to release them.

Let come to mind any self-judgment, self-recrimination, guilt, or anxiety you may be feeling over anything you said or did. It is very healing to clear these and not let them further affect you.

Is there anything else from today you could clear? Bring everything into the beautiful, radiant light of your divine Self until it reveals the nothingness of the energies you encountered and any that people projected onto you.

Picture going through your day tomorrow, being alert to the energy you are around and not accepting as your reality any thoughts, judgments, beliefs, or emotions that you do not want. Imagine divine perfection unfolding throughout the day as you experience and are able to sustain a clear, joyful state of being.

Clearing Thoughts about Your Physical Body

Throughout your lifetime you have accumulated a number of thoughts and beliefs about your body. It is important to be conscious of these thoughts and beliefs so you can let go of those you do not want to be your truth.

Pick an area of your physical body to work with in order to clear any negative thoughts and pictures you may have about it. This might be something such as your teeth, eyes, ears, nose, hair, bones, hands, feet, hips, heart, liver, kidneys, elbows, knees, ankles, weight, fitness level, general health, energy level, and so on. You might be amazed to discover how many negative, fearful thoughts you have about your body, which you have picked up from your culture, family, and friends, and from the media and the mass of general thoughts that exist "out there."

Make contact with your divine Self and shine Its radiant light on the part of your body you want to focus on. In this light, let surface any stories, thoughts, and feelings about this part of your body that would be to your benefit to release. What pictures do you have about how well this part of your body is working or not working? Are you giving energy to a possible problem that may occur in the future? How do you feel when you think about this area? Is there something you are afraid might go wrong in this area? What thoughts about aging might you hold in this part of your body?

You do not need to accept these concerns as your truth. As you release them, you will be dissipating the energy that these thoughts and beliefs might have and lessening the possibility that they will influence your health and well-being.

Shine your inner light on any concerns whenever they appear. These negative thoughts are not supported by any spiritual law. They are not showing you the true reality of your divine Self that shines forth from within you, radiating health and well-being. Recognize that these lesser thoughts have no power. They are just thoughts, and you do not need to give them energy. You do not have to clear all of them at once; you only need to clear those that come to mind.

Afterward, be open to any inner guidance showing you something you can do right now for greater health and physical well-being. Enjoy being in a clear state in which you are in touch with your body, open and listening to it. In this clear state you are responding only to the messages that come from your greater Self, and not those that come from mass consciousness. As you continue clearing lesser pictures of your body, you can enjoy better health, freedom from fear, and a sense of peace and well-being.

One man was told by his dentist that he needed to have some of his molars pulled because they were crowding out his other teeth and causing a lot of problems. The man's friends told him it would be painful to pull them out, which made him even less eager to get them removed. He also realized he was emotionally attached to his teeth and did not really want to let go of them.

After trying everything he could to save these teeth, he realized that having them pulled was his best option. He was determined to clear any fears or negative pictures about the procedure. He worked on releasing his attachment to these teeth, thanking them for their years of service and sending them love. He linked with his divine Self to clear any thoughts of pain and difficulty that others had told him to expect. He realized these were just thoughts that existed in mass consciousness and that this did not need to be his truth.

During the procedure, he connected with his divine Self and continued to reject negative thoughts. At the moment when the dentist pulled each tooth, he made a brief contact with his divine Self and held a positive picture of how easy it would be. To the great surprise of both his dentist and himself, the teeth came out so easily that they almost fell out. He had very little pain afterward and healed quickly.

Clearing Scarcity Thoughts

You can clear scarcity thinking in any area of your life where you are experiencing a shortage, such as a lack of money, sales, clients, business, jobs, ideas, contacts, friends, resources, or anything else you need. Clearing thoughts, memories, and feelings that stand in the way will make a big difference in your ability to create abundance.

Think of an area in which you would like to experience abundance. As you connect with your divine Self, sense your central channel of light shining out. Ask to become aware of any thoughts that are keeping you from experiencing abundance in the area you picked. Do you have thoughts that say you do not have what it takes, that something is wrong with you, or that you do not deserve to have abundance? Let these rise to the surface so you can release them by shining the light of your divine Self on them. Afterward, welcome the inspiring and encouraging thoughts that come into your mind to replace those based on lack and limitation. Enjoy these supportive thoughts and the inner guidance you can access when you are clear.

Let come to the surface any memories that may be holding you back from creating abundance. Clear old memories of lack and limitation. When you are clear, memories that arise will be supportive ones that show you your past successes and ability to create what you needed.

Let come to the surface whatever emotions that it is time to release. Perhaps you feel scared that you will fail or worried that you cannot handle success. Maybe you are afraid that having abundance will separate you from your friends and loved ones. Maybe you are afraid of change even if it is for the better, or you have other feelings coming up that have stood in the way of your ability to create abundance. These are your story and the reasons why you do not have abundance in that area of your life.

The light of your divine Self reveals that these memories, thoughts, and emotions can have no power over you and need no longer affect you. They do not reflect the truth of the divine being that you are. These limiting energies are not you; they are simply impersonal energies that come from mass consciousness. Observe them as they fade out and disappear in the light that you are holding.

Let yourself feel the freedom that clearing gives you to create a higher and more abundant life. When you clear scarcity thinking, you open the way for divine perfection to unfold, bringing you all that you need for your well-being and success. Thank your true, divine Self for all the abundance you already have and the abundance that is on its way to you.

An independent, intelligent woman who wanted to start her own business found much value in connecting with her divine Self and clearing energy to create success. She had found something she really loved to do. Her thoughts kept telling her she did not have what it took to succeed, because she did not have a college degree or any higher education. She had heard that the field was crowded and that she would have a hard time getting clients or having her products recognized. The general thought was that the field was highly competitive and she would need a lot of money, contacts, and experience to succeed. She knew she was very creative and resourceful, and she was determined to proceed, since she felt drawn to this field and wanted to be in it. She decided to clear these unwanted, limiting, fearful thoughts.

Instead, she believed that anything was possible if she was in touch with her innermost divine Self and stayed clear of the discouraging mass thoughts and beliefs that were all around. After facing and clearing many disheartening thoughts, she focused on positive, affirming thoughts that she could accomplish her goals and prosper in her business. She steadily focused on building a flourishing, profitable business. She followed her inner guidance and took many positive steps to succeed. She sought out and got the advice and knowledge she needed to be successful. She entertained only those thoughts and beliefs that empowered her and cleared those that did not. Even when she was faced with apparent setbacks, she kept releasing her doubts and fears and continued to picture and believe that things would work out.

She was able to do this by staying in constant contact with her divine Self throughout the day, with frequent short moments of pausing, getting quiet, and being open and receptive to the divine within her. After each contact she would receive a downflow of energy and guidance that led her to whatever she needed to do next to create a successful business. Contacts appeared, doors opened, and opportunities presented themselves. She reached and went beyond the goal she had set in her original vision, finding that each success opened her to another success.

Clearing Your Thoughts of Other People

You project many thoughts, images, and pictures onto other people, including your children, partner, spouse, parents, other relatives, friends, employees, employers, and so on. You can clear any images you have of others that may be holding them back. As you do this, you free people. You are no longer projecting energy onto them that they then have to clear.

Let someone come to mind that you have a lot of pictures, thoughts, or judgments about. Think of some picture you hold of this person that you would like to release, one that diminishes them in some way. Whatever you project on others is something within you that is holding you back. As you recognize the lesser thoughts and opinions you have of others and clear them, you are also clearing these for yourself, for all of these pictures are within your consciousness.

As you connect with your divine Self, radiate light to every negative thought or image that arises when you think of this person. Work only with those that come to mind, for these are the ones that are ready for you to release at this time. These negative images are not real, and they are not the truth of this person. You can let them go, freeing both of you.

As you release these images, perhaps think of this other person as if you have just met and you have no pictures or expectations of him or her. Feel the difference in the energy between both of you as you let go of past memories, judgments, and negative thoughts and images of him or her. Although you are not doing this to change the other person, he or she will be more likely to act in new ways as you release your old images. As you clear these, something will change in your relationship to the other person, and also in your relationship to yourself.

Clearing as a Process for Living an Earth Life

Every time you walk out the door, interact with others, or listen to or read the news, be alert to the negative, limiting beliefs, thoughts, and emotions that swirl around you. Anytime you hear about or read something that you do not want to become your reality, make a 10-second (longer is fine too!) connection to your divine Self. Recognize that these unwanted beliefs, thoughts, and emotions can have no power over you, for they are not backed by any spiritual law or truth. Feel your inner light shining through you as you illuminate these lower energies with your spiritual light. Let them disappear as you maintain a clear state.

Be alert when you are conversing with others, and pay attention to the images and thoughts they are projecting. If they are saying something you do not want to experience as your truth, such as "life is hard" or "people are uncaring," stay in a clear state and do not identify with or let these become your reality.

Watch what you say and speak of to others. Before you speak, note if you are passing along a thought or feeling that the other person will need to clear. You have the ability to lift others and assist them in getting clear.

You can use the clearing process in unlimited ways for everything you can think of. Be alert to what energies you choose to allow into your consciousness. You can have wonderful experiences, loving relationships, and physical and emotional well-being as you open to your divine Self and allow Its inner light to shine through you. Enjoy living a fulfilling life as you experience increasingly clear, happy, and peaceful states of higher consciousness.

Acknowledgments

From my heart I thank Orin for his unending patience, guidance, and wisdom. I thank my partner, Duane Packer, and his guide, DaBen, who have added many treasures of love, increased awareness, and spiritual growth to my life.

I especially thank all of you who are reading and working with *Personal Power through Awareness* for the contribution you are making to the world by becoming more aware of the subtle energies and how to work with them.

I extend my gratitude to those who helped us organize Orin's material and put it into this form: Edward Alpern for his many years of work with Orin and for his many contributions to *Personal Power*; LaUna Huffines, whose enthusiasm inspired me to channel this book; and to all those who have supported Orin's work through giving their time and energy to it, including family, friends, and LuminEssence staff.

I am very grateful to New World Library for their ongoing support of Orin's books, including Marc Allen, publisher;

Munro Magruder, associate publisher; Georgia Hughes, editorial director; Tracy Cunningham, cover designer; and all the other helpful staff there.

With deep gratitude, I thank the distributors and all the committed, dedicated bookstore owners and those who make Orin's books available through their websites and online stores — all of whom make it possible for Orin's books to reach you, the readers. I also thank our international publishers, who have made this information available around the world.

Companion Books by Orin and DaBen

Orin Books by Sanaya Roman

Living with Joy: 25th Anniversary Edition
Keys to Personal Power and Spiritual Transformation
Book 1 of the Earth Life Series

This book teaches you how to love and nurture yourself, live in higher purpose, and discover your life purpose. You will learn how to radiate love; be compassionate, tolerant, and forgiving; feel inner peace; take a quantum leap; gain clarity; open to new things; trust your inner guidance; change negatives into positives; and open to receive. You will learn to raise your vibration by increasing your ability to love; have more self-esteem; and create harmony, clarity, and peace. You can live with joy rather than struggle. Anniversary edition contains extensive new material!

Spiritual Growth: Being Your Higher Self
Book 3 of the Earth Life Series

This book will teach you how to reach upward and work with the higher powers of the Universe to accelerate your spiritual growth. You will learn how to link with the Higher

Will to flow with the Universe; connect with the Universal Mind for insights, enhanced creativity, and breakthroughs; expand your awareness of the inner planes; open your clairvoyant sight; receive revelations; and see the bigger picture of the Universe.

You will learn nonattachment, right use of will, and how to lift the veils of illusion. You will learn how to expand and contract time, choose your reality, become transparent, communicate in higher ways, and be your higher self. These tools will help you live your everyday life with more joy, harmony, peace, and love. This book will help you align with the higher energies that are coming and use them to live the best life you can imagine for yourself.

Soul Love:
Awakening Your Heart Centers

In *Soul Love*, you will meet and blend with your soul. You will learn more about your chakras and how to work with your soul and the Beings of Light to awaken your heart centers. When you awaken these centers, they work together in a triangle of light, and you can more easily experience soul love, peace, joy, bliss, and aliveness.

Discover how to attract a soul mate, make a soul link, make heart connections, create soul relationships, change personality love into soul love, and lift all the energies about you into your heart center to be purified and transformed. See results in your life when you use Orin's easy, step-by-step processes to heal your heart of past hurts, to open to receive more love, and to bring all your relationships to a higher level.

ORIN AND DABEN BOOKS BY
SANAYA ROMAN AND DUANE PACKER
Creating Money: Attracting Abundance

Learn how to follow the spiritual laws of abundance, use advanced manifesting techniques, and create what you want. You will discover how to draw your life's work to you. This book contains many simple techniques, positive affirmations, and exercises to help you create rapid changes in your prosperity.

Abundance is your natural state, and as you use the information in this book you will learn how to let money and abundance flow readily into your life while doing what you love. You can develop unlimited thinking, listen to your inner guidance, and transform your beliefs. Discover how to work with energy to create easily what you want and tap into the unlimited abundance of the Universe.

Opening to Channel:
How to Connect with Your Guide

Orin and DaBen, wise and healing spirit teachers channeled by Sanaya Roman and Duane Packer, will teach you how to connect with and verbally channel a high-level guide. Channeling is a skill that you can learn, and Sanaya and Duane have successfully trained thousands to channel using these safe, simple, and effective processes. You will learn what channeling is and how to know if you are ready to channel, how to get into a channeling state and receive information clearly, what to expect in your first meeting with your guide, and much more.

Sanaya Roman and Duane Packer • www.orindaben.com

Personal Power *Audio Courses by Orin*

A Message from Orin about Guided Meditations

I offer these guided meditations to you who have read my books and want to go further, using and living these principles. Working with guided meditations, where your mind is in a relaxed, open state, is a powerful way to create rapid, profound, and lasting changes in your life. I have carefully selected the processes, words, and images used in these meditations to awaken you to your true, innermost Self. These guided meditations will teach you how to expand your consciousness so you can become more aware of and influence the energy you live in and around. I offer these meditations to you who want to take a quantum leap, become more aware of subtle energy, and create a harmonious life.

Personal Power Through Awareness *Audio Courses*

Listen to these audio courses to further your ability to sense energy and put into practice what is taught in the book.

Personal Power Through Awareness — Part 1: Sensing Energy. Create the reality you want using energy, thought, and light. Develop your skills of visualizing, sensing, and affecting the energy around you; of increasing your intuitive abilities and your ability to receive higher guidance. Includes: **Sensing Energy; Sensing Unseen Energy; Sensing Energy in Others; Who Am I? — Sensing Your Own Energy; Developing Intuition; Evolving Emotional Telepathy; Sending and Receiving Telepathic Images;** and **Receiving Higher Guidance.** 8 meditations by Orin with music by Thaddeus. (P201)

Personal Power Through Awareness — Part 2: Journey Into Light. Experience yourself in new, higher ways, be in your power, remain centered when you are around others, and more. The processes in this course contain powerful techniques to evolve and uplift your experience of yourself and your life. Includes: **Learning Unconditional Love; Handling Pain — Transforming Negative Energy; Bringing Your Unconscious into Consciousness; Journey into Light — Going Higher; Self-Love — Evolving Your Inner Dialogue; Transforming Your Inner Images; Finding Your Deepest Truth;** and **Wisdom — Being Your Higher Self.** 8 meditations by Orin with music by Thaddeus. (P202)

Orin's Audio Courses to Further Expand Your Personal Power and Clear Energy

Orin's Divine Self Series: Work with your innermost, divine Self in the following audio courses by Orin. Awaken to the truth of who you are, a spiritual being living an earth life.

Clearing Energy with Your Divine Self *Audio Course*

Listen to guided meditations to expand upon what you learned in chapters 17–19 in the *Personal Power* book. Open to the illumination of your divine, innermost Self, which clears energy that may veil your inner light, such as fears, emotions, beliefs, thoughts, other people's expectations, memories, and energy that comes from mass consciousness.

Discover more about the nature of the energy you are clearing and how to stay in the clearest states possible, no matter what kind of energy you are around. When you are clear, you can sense and follow your inner guidance and discern your highest path. When you are clear, you feel good about yourself; you are more joyful, insightful, inspired, focused, and confident.

Meditations include all of the meditations in the "Clearing Suggestions" in chapter 19 of the *Personal Power* book and many more. 20 Orin meditations and PDF manual with much additional information on how to effectively clear energy. (DS203)

Knowing Your True Identity *Audio Course*

Open to know who you really are — a Self who has everything you need within you. When you realize what a vast consciousness you are, you no longer feel like a small, powerless, separate self. You gain more confidence and self-esteem. You are able to handle situations with greater wisdom, insight, and love. 12 Orin meditations. (DS201)

Awakening Your Spiritual Power *Audio Course*

Explore the truth that there is only one power, that of the Self within you. Discover what it means to live this truth as you open to the realization that nothing can have power over you, the true Self. With this realization you can shift any situation for the better as you work with light and energy. Experience the divine consciousness of your innermost Self as *your* consciousness. 12 Orin meditations. (DS202)

Opening to Channel *Audio Courses*
How to Connect With Your Guide

These channeling courses by Sanaya and Duane will assist you in making a connection with and learning how to channel or receive inner messages from a guide or your higher self.

Sanaya and Duane, with the assistance of their guides, Orin and DaBen, have successfully trained thousands to make a connection to their guides and bring through useful information and guidance using these safe, simple, and effective processes. Channeling courses are available in printed, ebook, and audiobook formats on our website. OTC

Updated and Revised
Opening to Channel *Audio Meditations*

This audio course is a wonderful companion to the *Opening to Channel* book. It contains the processes taught by Sanaya and Duane at their *Opening to Channel* seminars, as well as chapters on how to give readings from the *Opening to Channel* book, read by Sanaya. As you listen, Orin and DaBen will lead you through each step of channeling, including relaxation, concentration, mentally meeting your guide, and learning to channel verbally if you choose. Processes include many channeling state inductions to make a stronger connection to your guide, tune in to another person, give yourself a reading, and see out into time. 25 programs; includes talks and guided meditations by Orin and DaBen. (C101)

Orin's Channeling Your Guide:
Receiving Clear Guidance

This channeling course will strengthen your ability to recognize that a guide is really present, and go from there to greatly expand your ability to receive guidance. You will learn how to deal with doubts that you are really channeling as you explore and learn more about your guide. In the second part of this course you will expand your ability to get clear guidance, such as through looking into time, expanding on the details, and seeing the bigger picture of whatever you want more information about. This course was made to lift you above the doubts and concerns that are common in learning to channel. You can receive all the gifts that await you with this connection. This course is helpful for any level of skill in channeling to increase your ability to receive accurate, clear guidance from your guide. Orin course, 12 meditations. (C201)

Awakening Your Light Body:
Keys to Enlightenment

Explore One of Our Most Transformative
Energy-Sensing Audio Courses

The *Awakening Your Light Body* courses offer a unique path of spiritual awakening through experiential, progressive expansions of consciousness that assist you in directly knowing the truth of your being.

Orin joins with DaBen (channeled by Duane Packer) to present *Awakening Your Light Body,* an audio course that will assist you in experiencing heightened states of consciousness as you expand into higher realms and experience yourself as you exist there. Each meditation expands upon the one before to take you step-by-step into very flowing, insightful, and clear states of awareness. Course contains extensive written material and 74 audio meditations in six volumes. It offers you a program of spiritual growth and Self-realization that comes from directly experiencing higher states. This path of study is recommended for you if you have been on a growth path for a while, want to experience many heightened, expanded states of consciousness, and want to increase your ability to sense and work with subtle spiritual energies.

What Is Your Light Body?

Your light body is an energy body that exists beyond the level of the chakras and your soul. As you awaken it, you can experience higher states of consciousness, change less harmonious energies into harmonious ones, create flowing emotions and clear, insightful thoughts, and open your channel upward to your guide and to the higher aspects of your being.

As you awaken your higher light body centers, you become radiant with light. You can experience many illumined states of awareness. These states of consciousness can feel deeply peaceful, blissful, and take you beyond thought into direct experiences of beingness. We also have many graduate light body courses to assist you in expanding into even higher states. Extensive information about this course is available on our website. (LB111-LB116)

Orin's Vision Courses

In the two Vision courses, Orin links you with Star energies from the Great Bear, Pleiades, Sirius, and the Spiritual Sun for transformation and to greatly expand your ability to sense energy.

In **Part 1**, *Vision: Seeing and Sensing Subtle Energies*, you will learn how to awaken your third eye to see and sense subtle energies as you work with star energies. Learn to see beyond illusions, without doubt, fear, or emotions that cloud inner vision. Develop etheric vision and clear your aura. Sense the energy of your higher purpose, better know what to manifest, and follow your path of spiritual growth. (OR917)

In **Part 2**, *Vision: Creating Your Highest Future*, you will discover ways to look into time, to find the future you are now creating, and to create an even better, higher future. Use this course to find those choices, decisions, and paths that will bring you a fulfilling life. Read your soul's records to learn more about your soul's purpose for being on earth. Unfold your higher potential and live your life purpose. (OR918)

Personal Power *Audio Short Course*

Orin offers these two audio programs to further develop your awareness of subtle, unseen energy. Program 1 contains affirmations, and Program 2 contains a guided meditation. (P100)

Single Meditations

- **Developing Intuition** (O10) • **Telepathy** (O15)
- **Opening Up Psychic Abilities** (O13)
- **Opening Your Chakras** (O16) • **Lucid Dreaming** (SI024)
- **Trusting Your Inner Guidance** (SI107)
- **Taking a Quantum Leap** (L103)
- **Meeting Your Spirit Guide** (O14)
- **Age Regression** (SI041) • **Past-Life Regression** (SI043)
- **Discovering Your Life Purpose** (L104)
- **For Self-Employed: Creating Money, Clients, Sales** (SI037)
- **Opening to Receive** (L106) • **Self-Love** (L102)
- **Radiating Unconditional Love** (P103)
- **Feeling Energetic** (SI005) • **Body Beautiful** (SI050)
- **Losing Weight, Looking Younger** (SI030)
- **Attracting Your Soul Mate** (RE002)
- **Having What You Want in a Relationship** (RE003)

Creating Money *Audio Course*

Reprogram your subconscious to create more abundance in your life. The meditations in this series include: **Magnetizing Yourself** (SI010); **Clearing Beliefs and Old Programs** (SI071); **Releasing Doubts and Fears** (SI075); **Linking with Your Soul and the Guides** (SI076); **Aura Clearing, Energy, and Lightwork** (SI073); **Awakening Your Prosperity Self** (SI074); **Success** (SI070); and **Abundance** (SI072). These can either be purchased separately or as a set. All 8 meditations (M100).

Creating Money audiobook available on our website. (CME)

Living Your Life Purpose *Audio Course*

Learn how to live your purpose in each moment. View your life purpose through the perspective of your higher self and soul to learn more about it. Explore how to call upon beings of light for strength and courage, and to empower you to find and live your life purpose.

Receive energy from a Great One, a being of great light, to gain clarity and insight into the higher purpose of various areas of your life. Evolve your personality so that it can better carry out the goals of your higher self and soul. Have greater clarity about what activities you are doing that are in alignment with your higher purpose, and those that are not. 8 Orin meditations, music by Thaddeus. (OR914)

Becoming a Writer *Audio Course*

These powerful meditations contain the processes given to Sanaya by Orin to help get their books out to the world. Meditations include: **I Am a Writer; Manifesting Your Writing; Loving to Write; Connecting With Your Audience;** and processes to get your writing published. 4 meditations by Orin, music by Thaddeus. (SI016)

Receive a Free Newsletter

Visit our website to subscribe to our free printed newsletter, sent twice a year, with information and articles you may enjoy.

Sign up with your email to receive our online eNewsletters (not the same as our printed newsletter) with links to free new Orin audio meditations and much more.

Orin's Living with Joy *Book*

25th Anniversary Edition
* New Additional Information * Over 300 new Joy Affirmations
* 18 new Daily Joy Practices for an uplifting day

Living with Joy teaches you how to feel and express the joy of your soul. You can grow through joy and release pain and struggle. You will explore ways to feel inner peace no matter what is happening, experience more freedom, change negatives into positives, trust your inner guidance, gain clarity, open to the new, and feel the joy of your soul in your everyday life. Available in print, ebook, and audiobook formats. LWJ

Orin's Living with Joy *Audio Meditations*

Living with Joy — The Path of Joy, Part 1: Audio course by Orin to sound your soul's note of joy and bring more joy into your life. Meditations include: **Finding Your Path of Joy; Changing Negatives into Positives; The Art of Self-Love; Self-Worth and Self-Esteem; Power — Refining Your Ego; Knowing Your Heart's Wisdom; Opening to Receive;** and **Appreciation and Gratitude**. 8 meditations by Orin, Thaddeus music. (L201)

Living with Joy — Taking a Quantum Leap, Part 2: Audio course by Orin. Meditations include: **Finding Inner Peace; Balance and Stability; Clarity — Living in the Light; Freedom; Embracing the New; Taking a Quantum Leap; Living in Higher Purpose;** and **Recognizing Life Purpose**. 8 meditations by Orin (L202)

Living with Joy *Audio Short Course*

Bring the principles of the *Living with Joy* book into your daily life with this audio course. (L100)
Program 1 — Affirmations • Program 2 — Guided Meditation

Single Meditations to Assist You in Growing with Joy

- **Feeling Inner Peace** (L101) • **Self-Love** (L102)
- **Opening to Receive** (L106) • **Balance and Stability** (L105)
- **Becoming Self-Confident** (RE008)
- **Handling Anxiety and Fear** (SI063)
- **Reprogramming at a Cellular Level** (SI056)
- **Clearing Blockages** (SI057) • **Creating Your Perfect Day** (SI101)
- **Overcoming the Self-Destruct** (SI060)
- **Losing Weight, Looking Younger** (SI030)

LuminEssence Productions • www.orindaben.com

Orin's Spiritual Growth *Book*

Being Your Higher Self

Spiritual Growth, the third book of Orin's Earth Life Series, teaches you how to develop an integrated, balanced personality called your higher self, one who knows and can carry out the goals and purposes of your soul. You will learn how to link with the Higher Will to flow with the Universe; connect with the Universal Mind for insights, enhanced creativity, and breakthroughs; receive revelations; and see the bigger picture of the Universe.

You will learn nonattachment, right use of will, and how to lift the veils of illusion. You will discover how to expand and contract time, choose your reality by working with probable futures, become transparent to energy you do not like, and be your higher self. Available in printed, ebook, and audiobook formats. SG

Orin's Spiritual Growth *Audio Meditations*

Spiritual Growth — Raising Your Vibration, Part 1: Guided meditations for: **Raising Your Vibration; Calming Your Emotions; Accelerating Your Spiritual Growth; Choosing Your Reality; Expanding and Contracting Time; Lifting the Veils of Illusion; Right Use of Will;** and **Becoming Transparent.** 8 meditations by Orin. (SG101)

Spiritual Growth — Being Your Higher Self, Part 2: Guided meditations for: **Being Your Higher Self; Creating With Light; Connecting With the Universal Mind; Linking With the Higher Will; Seeing the Bigger Picture; Opening Awareness of the Inner Planes; Allowing Your Higher Good;** and **Nonattachment.** 8 meditations by Orin, music by Thaddeus. (SG102)

Spiritual Growth *Audio Short Course*

Bring the principles of the *Spiritual Growth* book into your daily life with this short audio course. (SG200)
Program 1 — Affirmations • Program 2 — Guided Meditation
Also available: Single guided meditation — Being Your Higher Self (SI040)

Visit our website for ordering information, media formats available, cost, and more. Enjoy lots of free and fun things to do, listen to free full-length meditations by Orin, get daily affirmations, and much more.

Orin's Asking and Receiving from Your Divine Self *Audio Course*

Orin created this course to assist you in opening to the infinite possibilities for good that await you in every area of your life. You will learn how to connect with your divine Self, then explore all the energy you can ask for and receive. You no longer need to live with lack or limitation. You ask for so much less than you can have. Learn to recognize that you can ask for and receive far more than you ever dreamed possible! 13 audio guided meditations and a PDF manual with much additional information. (DS204)

Orin's Soul Love *Audio Course*

In Orin's *Soul Love,* you will meet and blend with your soul and awaken your heart center to experience soul love, peace, joy, bliss, and aliveness. See results in your life when you use Orin's easy, step-by-step processes to heal your heart of past hurts and open to receive more love.

Volume 1: Soul Love — Awakening Your Heart Centers. Meditations include: **Making Soul Contact; Blending With Your Soul; Soul Linking; The Serenity of Love; The Oneness of Love; The Will to Love; Surrendering to Love;** and **Soul Love.** 8 meditations. (SL105)

Volume 2: Creating a Soul Relationship. Work soul-to-soul to transform a relationship. Meditations include: **Meeting Soul to Soul; Light Play; Love Play; Creating the Relationship You Want; Dissolving Obstacles to Love; Discovering New Ways to Love;** and **Soul Blending.** 8 meditations by Orin (SL106)

Transformation: Evolving Your Personality *Audio Course*

Move through challenges that come from being on an accelerated path of spiritual growth, such as blockages, doubts, old issues coming up, overstimulation, and so on. Meditations include: **Self-Appreciation; Honoring Your Path of Awakening; Focusing Inward — Hearing Your Soul's Voice; Focusing Upward — Hearing the Voice of the Masters and Guides; Reparenting Yourself; Creating the Future with Light; Beyond Intellect — Opening Your Higher Mind;** and **Journey to the Temple of the Masters to Reprogram at a Cellular Level.** 8 guided meditations by Orin (SG200)

Explore Orin's Millennium/Star Journeys
Expand Every Level of Your Being

The guided meditation audio courses by Orin that follow can assist you in accelerating your spiritual growth. Orin links you with Star energies from the Great Bear, Pleiades, Sirius, and the Spiritual Sun for transformation. These guided meditations can expand your consciousness, accelerate your evolution, and illuminate your mind. Each course contains 12 Orin meditations with music by Thaddeus.

Volume 1: Increasing Your Inner Light. Your inner light determines what you experience and draw to you. Increase your inner light by working with star energy. You can release anything that does not support you, and draw to you your higher good. Surround yourself with light; awaken your soul vision and ability to sense the future; and experience more of your soul's light, love, will, power, serenity, and joy. (MM010)

Volume 2: Expanding Your Consciousness. Open to star energy to align with purpose at the highest of levels. Receive energy from the beings of light, awaken your chakras, manifest your higher path, stay in the flow, and become a light for others. Open your intuition and channel. (MM020)

Volume 3: Accelerating Your Evolution. Link with your soul and connect with the light of Spirit to accelerate your evolution. Explore soul vision; gain new insights and perspectives; let your body, mind, and emotions come to a higher vibration; know and express your inner truth; and release attachments, limitations, and energy blockages. (MM030)

Volume 4: Building a Radiant Aura. Work with the angel of the devas — small angelic beings — to build a radiant aura. Your radiance determines the situations and circumstances of your life, and the type of energy you live in and around. You will purify your aura of negative energies, and create an aura filled with light and star energy. (MM040)

Transcending Your Ego *Audio Courses*

Orin's meditations in this series are uplifting and expansive, guiding you to experience the illumination of your Divine Self. Become aware of your ego and rise above it to a new, higher consciousness. You can evolve your ego and change your thoughts, emotions, and daily life for the better. All courses in this series contain 12 guided meditations by Orin.

Volume 1: Birthing a New You. Are you ready to experience your life and consciousness in new ways, to know more joy, love, peace, harmonious relationships, and abundance? Are you ready to know the magnificence of your Divine Self as who you are? Includes: **Opening to Your Divine Self; Awakening Your Spiritual Power; Trusting Your Inner Wisdom; Calling Upon Divine Self Inspiration; Transforming Limiting Thoughts; Experiencing More Freedom in Your Life; Tapping Into Infinite Supply; Receiving Divine Self Guidance; Knowing the Peace of Your Divine Self; Rising Into Divine Consciousness; Enjoying Harmonious Relationships;** and **Birthing a New You.** (DS101)

Volume 2: Transforming Your Emotions. Connect with your divine Self to release negative emotions. As the fogs of strong emotions dissipate in the light of your divine Self, a path opens up into many higher states of consciousness that are only possible to experience with flowing and peaceful emotions. Includes: **Awakening Divine Love; Staying Clear Around Negative Emotions; Creating Positive Emotions About Your Body; Changing a Situation by Freeing Stuck Emotions; Dissolving Blockages to Divine Self Contact; Clearing Obstacles to Experiencing Infinite Supply; Choosing the Rewards of a Peaceful Life; Loving Yourself by Refusing Negative Emotions; Freeing Yourself From Repeating the Past; Releasing Pain; Deepening and Sustaining Inner Peace;** and **Accepting More Peace, Joy, and Love.** (DS102)

Volume 3: Evolving Your Desire Body. Evolve your desire body so that it responds to Divine Will and to your divine Self rather than to mass consciousness or other people's desires. Create circumstances that fulfill you. Experience yourself as radiant light, love, and wisdom. Includes: **Increasing Your Desire for Divine Self Contact; Reorienting Your Desire Body; Aligning Your Desires With Higher Purpose; Freeing Yourself From Unfulfilling Desires; Becoming Pure Awareness Without Desire; Evolving Your Desire Body; Exploring Your New Desire Body; Releasing Past Desires; Opening to the Opportunity in Each Moment; Accelerating Your Transformation; Elevating All the Energies About You;** and **Living an Inspired Life.** (DS103)

Volume 4: Illuminating Your Mind. Experience pure awareness — states of stillness where you can receive creative thoughts and clear inner guidance. Your thoughts will then show you the way and bring you peace and solutions. Includes: **Experiencing the Light That Reveals the Mind; Realizing the True Nature of Thoughts; Rising Above Mind-Chatter; Responding to Your Thoughts in New Ways; Letting Go of Worry Thoughts; Freeing Yourself From Limiting Beliefs; Dissolving Fixed Opinions: Awakening Divine Vision; Strengthening Divine Self Guidance; Connecting With the Divine Self of Others; Receiving Divine Ideas: Opening to New Possibilities; Releasing Limiting Thoughts About Your Body and Aging;** and **Illuminating Your Mind.** (DS104)

Volume 5: Deepening Divine Self Consciousness. Experience the great, revealing, illuminating light of your divine Self. This illumination makes it possible to transcend your ego in even more profound, life-changing ways. The sun of the Self radiates Its light into your mind, desires, and emotions, into anywhere you have been closed, limited, or stuck. It frees you! Includes: **Breaking Through to New Consciousness; Becoming Pure Awareness Without Thoughts; Coming into Resonance With Your Divine Self; Experiencing a New You: Letting Go of Old Identities; Updating the Roles You Play; Asking and Receiving From Your Divine Self; Knowing Your Formless Self; Freeing Yourself From Past Labels; Into the Light: Clearing the Storms of Emotions; Being True to Your Self; Recognizing the Divine in Others;** and **Embracing Your New Identity.** (DS105)

Volume 6: Transcending Your Ego. Experience many wonderful states of illumination where lesser thoughts and desires release themselves from you. Emotions become more balanced, flowing, and peaceful. Experience what a gift it is, what joy, when the clouds of the ego part and the light of your divine Self bursts forth from within you. There is a feeling of well-being, as if you are lifting out of the darkness into the light of day. Includes: **Stabilizing Your Emotions; Experiencing Desirelessness; Receiving Gifts of Consciousness; Rising Above Your Ego; Freeing Yourself From Attachments; Practicing Self-Forgiveness; Releasing the Need to Suffer; Moving Beyond Needing Approval; Letting Things Be; Responding As Your Divine Self; Allowing a New Consciousness to Arise;** and **Radiating Your Inner Beauty.** (DS106)

Visit our website for more information, media formats available, and more product information.

Orin's Divine Will *Audio Courses*
Manifesting with Divine Will

Become a master of manifesting by linking with each of the seven Great Ones who hold and radiate Divine Will. Discover the inner space from which all divine manifesting is done — a place of illumination, in contact with your divine Self. As you connect with the consciousness of your divine Self and the seven Divine Wills, you gain the ability to create whatever you feel guided to do, building a blueprint in the higher realms that can then appear in your life as harmonious, positive circumstances.

Divine manifesting is about creating a life you love, with satisfying relationships, pleasurable activities, and joyful work. It involves creating a life of joy, love, harmony, peace, inspiration, wholeness, and freedom. Contains audio and a booklet with extensive information about divine manifesting. (DW917)

Transforming Your Life with Divine Will

Stop struggling to change your life and accomplish your goals. Instead, receive energy from the Great Ones who radiate the seven qualities of Divine Will. Change your life and consciousness in wonderful ways without struggle or using the force of your personal will to create what you want.

You can open to receive Divine Will and draw it into your life for insights and revelations; to evolve your consciousness, release limitations, align with your higher mind for inspiration and creativity; to stop conflict and experience peace and harmony. 12 audio meditations and written material. (MM050)

Living a Soul Life with Divine Will

You can call upon the power of Divine Will to live as your soul. You will learn how to link with all seven Divine Wills to live as your soul through experiencing divine love, both for yourself and others. Living as your soul transforms your emotions, illuminates your mind, brings a greater sense of physical well-being, and allows you to better know and live your soul's purpose. Experience the abundance and creativity of your soul, receive its clear guidance, create a supportive environment, and live a soul life. 12 audio meditations by Orin and written material. (MM060)

Enjoy Many Free and Fun Things to Do on Our Website at www.orindaben.com

Come visit our website and enjoy connecting with us. You can have fun in various ways and be uplifted and inspired:

- **Read** more about Orin and Sanaya Roman.
- **Sign our guestbook** and let us know about you!
- Read extensive **information about creating money** and abundance.
- Read **information about channeling** and how to know if you are ready.
- Read **articles by Orin** on various topics.
- Read free **weekly meditations and weekly book excerpts.**
- Go to our Creating Your Highest Future room, click on any book cover, and **receive daily guidance from Orin's books.**
- Listen to **free online Orin meditations** on topics such as self-love, clearing blockages, clear and creative thinking, receiving solar light, increasing soul vision, making soul contact, receiving abundance, relaxation, feeling energized, loving relationships, radiating unconditional love, cellular activation, and more.
- Get **daily affirmations** on creating money and abundance, loving relationships, losing weight, health and well-being, clearing blockages, increasing psychic abilities and intuition, opening your channel, loving yourself, and more.
- Sanaya works with an angelic being named Thaddeus to create beautiful angelic music. You can **listen to free Thaddeus' music samples** online.

Free Orin Newsletters and eNewsletters

Visit our website and subscribe to our free printed newsletter containing articles, affirmations, and information about Orin's audio courses and books. We offer eNewsletters sent to you several times a year (not the same as our printed newsletter) if we have your email address. These contain links to free Orin audio meditations and articles.

Contact Us

Sanaya Roman
LuminEssence Productions
www.orindaben.com

Visit Our Website for Free and Fun Things to Do

Sign our guestbook, and let us know about you. Enjoy listening to free Orin audio meditations, receive daily affirmations, read weekly book excerpts and articles, relax with special music created by Sanaya, and more. Explore Orin's path of self-realization offered through his books and audio courses. Subscribe to our free printed newsletter; each one has articles and exercises for your spiritual growth. We offer eNewsletters (not the same as our printed newsletter), sent to you several times a year if we have your email address, containing links to new free Orin audio meditations and articles of interest.